D0432687

Knit a FANTASY STORY

Other Search Press books by Jan Messent

Have You any Wool?
Wool 'n Magic

Needle Crafts series
Stitchery
Embroidery Design

Craft Library series
Knitted Gnomes and Fairies
Knit an Enchanted Castle
Knit the Christmas Story

Knit a FANTASY STORY

Jan Messent

SEARCH PRESS
in association with
CHILD & ASSOCIATES and DAVID BATEMAN
Australia   New Zealand

First published in Great Britain 1989
Search Press Ltd
Wellwood, North Farm Road,
Tunbridge Wells, Kent TN2 3DR
 In association with
Child & Associates Pty Ltd
5 Skyline Place
Frenches Forest
NSW, Australia 2086
  and
David Bateman Ltd
Golden Heights
32–34 View Road
Glenfield
Auckland, New Zealand

Based on the following volumes of the Craft Library series,
published by Search Press Limited:

The Knitted Farmyard. Original German version
Spiellandschaft aus Wolle (No 200 in the Brunnen-Reihe
series) copyright © 1982 Christophorus-Verlag Gmbh,
Freiburg im Breisgau. English version copyright © 1985
Search Press Limited. Original text and designs by
Hannelore Wernhard; translated by Hilary Simpson, re-
written and with new drawings by Jan Messent;
photographs by Ulrike Schneiders.

Knit an Enchanted Castle by Jan Messent

Knitted Gnomes and Fairies by Jan Messent

ISBN 0 85532 643 3 (C)
ISBN 0 85532 640 9 (pb)

Typeset by Scribe Design, 123 Watling Street, Gillingham,
Kent
Made and printed in Spain by Artes Graphicas Elkar S.
Coop. Autonamia, 71 - 48012-Bilbao - Spain.

CONTENTS

Introduction   6

Tools, materials and sizes   9

Abbreviations, stitches and symbols   11

Farmyard fantasia   13

Landscape   14

Buildings   16

Figures   18

Animals   27

Enchanted castle   37

Castle   38

Figures and animals   42

Magic forest   59

Forest   60

Figures   64

Animals   85

Helping hand   94

Index   95

INTRODUCTION

Enter a world of make-believe; an enchanted world of witches and wizards, fairies and goblins, bold knights, dragons, trolls and unicorns. The sleepy little farm nestles snugly under the hills, looking out over the enchanted forest, where fairies and gnomes work and play. Inside the huge stone castle lives the handsome prince, who will one day find his beautiful princess and take her to live there in safety, far away from the mischievous plottings of the wicked witch.

Well, that's the beginning of the story!

What happens along the way can be made with the help of an active imagination, these patterns and a little time and patience. Fairy stories are as popular today as they have ever been in the past, delighting both children and adults. Naturally, your attempt to create this enchanted land must rely partly on your own ideas and partly on suggestions found in literature and art. We have made this book of make-believe in a truly three-dimensional way to delight anyone with a sense of fantasy and fun.

The scale of the models is probably the most important element of the project, so seek out your finest needles, hooks and yarn and enjoy working in miniature. The tallest of the figures is approximately 5 in/14 cm tall. The base of the farm is the size of a small rug, although it can be made larger if you wish. The castle rises 16 in/41 cm to the tops of the pointed roofs and its base is the size of a large dinner plate.

The farm is built up using a mixture of knitting and crochet, although all the main pieces are knitted. The quantities of materials required are quite small; oddments of knitting yarns, rug canvas and embroidery threads, synthetic padding and pipe cleaners. The enchanted castle and the forest are made out of wool, cardboard tubes, card and wire.

All the figures are based on a wire frame and therefore make unsuitable toys for very young children, as they may be dangerous if not handled carefully. For practical reasons the clothes are not intended to be removed.

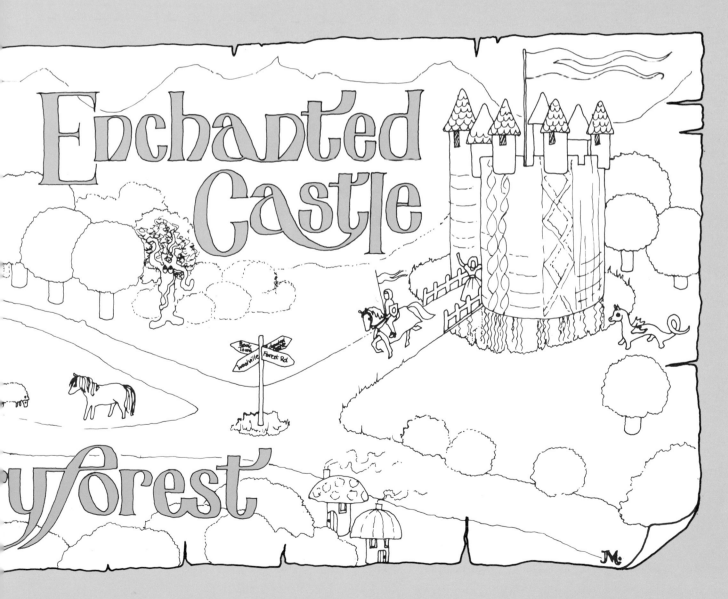

In the patterns they fit tightly without fastenings and the fairy folk have their wings sewn firmly on to their backs, so securing their clothes.

Although most of the knitting is on a small scale the instructions are not complex. The shapes used for body coverings and clothes are simple and are mostly based on rectangles or triangles, with occasional increasing and decreasing. Even the castle is made from straight pieces of knitting and would be an excellent project for a group of people to make together.

Use your imagination to add props and backgrounds to your enchanted land. Dolls' house accessories would be ideal. Oddments and scraps could add new dimensions to your knitted landscape. Young and old alike will enjoy hours of pleasure and fun while creating this land of fantasy and enchantment.

Specific details of the materials required and the methods of working each figure are given in the instructions but it is impossible to give exact details of the finished sizes, as this will depend on the yarn and needle size you use and the tension you obtain.

Needles

Requirements are given in the instructions for individual models but, generally, very fine needles are used throughout. It is sometimes easier to find these in sets of four double-pointed needles, rather than in pairs. These are perfectly adequate as only a few stitches are used for most projects. Fine Shetland 'wires', also found in sets of four, are used to create some of the garments for the fairy folk.

Other requirements include stitch holders and row counters, blunt-ended needles for sewing with wool, (tapestry needles) and a fine crochet hook.

Yarns

Requirements are given in the instructions for individual models, although the colours are your own personal choice. Only small amounts of two, three and four ply are normally needed but double knitting qualities have been used for the enchanted castle and the forest.

Use the very finest yarns you can find for the fairy folk. Glittering metallic yarns add sparkle and magic to an elf or pixie. Mohair mixtures are suitable for hair and beards and you will also need a thick yarn for wrapping around the frames of the figures. Textured and marbled yarns, such as bouclé and tweed, are ideal for the animals. Oddments of suitable colours will also be required for embroidering features and adding minute details.

The knitted body covering for the inhabitants of the Fantasy Story needs to be worked in a fine, smooth yarn. The illustrations will indicate suitable colouring but if you cannot obtain a pleasing flesh tone, use white two-ply dipped in strong tea or coffee. Wind off a hank, tie it in two or three places to prevent it becoming tangled, then dip in hot or cold tea or coffee for anything from ten to thirty minutes. Keep checking until you have the shade you require but remember that the colour will appear darker when wet.

Wire

Pipe cleaners are used as the basic framework for all the characters and 11in/28cm of thicker, but bendy wire, is needed for the fairy wings. Strong, bendable wire is required for the talking trees. You will also need wire cutters and a small pair of pliers.

Padding and card

Padding is needed for the animals, toadstools, talking trees and to pad out any very stout figures, such as the gnome or goblin. The cardboard tubes inside toilet rolls, also larger tubes approximately 9in/23cm high are needed and small pieces of thick card for stands.

Extras

Pencils and rulers are useful, as are tape measures, glue, adhesive tape (also double-sided), sharp scissors and lots of patience!

All kinds of extras may be added as the fancy takes you. Brighten up the fairy folk with tiny beads and sequins. Buckles, buttons, broken jewellery and gold and silver cord and braid will all add a touch of sparkle, so look in your 'bit box'. Anything small enough will most certainly have a use.

Sizes and tension

Please note that all the instructions given in this book are merely guidelines and will almost certainly have to be altered here and there to fit figures and shapes of all sizes, as no two people ever work to exactly the same tension. You may have to add or subtract a few stitches and/or rows and if a different weight of yarn is used from the one recommended, then a bit of juggling is inevitable!

It is therefore vital to check your knitted pieces against the model you have made, to make sure that each bit fits before the garment is sewn up.

ABBREVIATIONS, STITCHES, SYMBOLS

Most of the items in this book are knitted in stocking stitch, made by knitting and purling alternate rows. The other side of this fabric is known as 'reverse stocking stitch'. Garter stitch is formed by knitting every row.

Other knitting, crochet and general abbreviations are as follows:

alt	alternate(ly)
beg	begin(ning)
cm	centimetre(s)
ch	crochet chains
ch sp	chain space
dec	decrease
dc	double crochet (US, single crochet)
DK	double knitting yarn
foll	following
gt s	garter stitch
gm	gramme(s)
in	inch(es)
inc	increase
k	knit
k 2 tog	knit 2 together to decrease
LH	left hand
k-wise	in a knitwise direction
M1	make 1 by picking up loop
mm	millimetre(s)
No	number
oz	ounce(s)
patt	pattern
pc	pipe cleaner(s)
p	purl
p 2 tog	purl 2 together to decrease
p-wise	in a purlwise direction
psso	pass slipped stitch over
rev ss	reversed stocking stitch
rem	remain(ing)
rep	repeat
RS	right side of fabric
sl	slip
st	stitch(es)
ss	stocking stitch
tog	together
WS	wrong side of fabric
y fwd	yarn forward
yrn	yarn round needle

Stitches used

Double moss stitch
Garter stitch
Moss stitch
Other stitches of own choice
Picot stitch
Reversed stocking stitch
Single rib
Stocking stitch

Symbols used

A single asterisk, *, in the row indicates that the stitches following this sign are to be repeated as directed.

Instructions given in round brackets, ( ), are repeated as many times as indicated in the instructions.

FARMYARD FANTASIA

*The farmer and his family work all day
beneath the shade of the magic forest,
protected by the enchanted castle.*

LANDSCAPE

This colourful setting is a wonderful landscape for your farmyard fantasy.

Rug base

Copy the rug diagram opposite, full-scale, on to a large piece of brown paper, and use this as a pattern for the rug canvas work. Place it underneath the canvas and draw on to this with a thick fibre pen. You will need rug canvas measuring 52 × 35½ in/130 × 90 cm, plus an extra 2¼ in/6 cm all round for turning under.

Yarns: thick knitting wools, rug-thrums and cut rug-wool will be most useful for the base, part of which is covered with tufting and some with stitchery (see Figs 1 and 2).

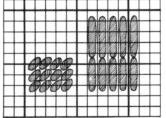

Fig 1:
left, tent stitch
right, satin stitch over
three and four threads
of the canvas

Fig 2:
tufting on rug canvas may
be done with a latchet hook,
or with a crochet hook

COLOURS AND STITCHES

Meadows: pale green 4 in/10 cm lengths of yarn knotted into the canvas as shown in Fig 1.

Street and yard: grey/beige double-thickness yarn embroidered in tent st.

Ploughed fields: several different browns, knitted in single rib to the shapes of the pattern and sewn on to the canvas.

Cornfields: several different yellows, as follows:

Ripe corn: 7 in/18 cm lengths of double yarn in deep yellow, and knotted.

Cornfield 1: knotted with 6¼ in/16 cm lengths of deep green yarn, doubled.

Cornfield 2: two tones of green yarn, 7¾ in/20 cm long, knotted.

Cornfield 3: double yarn in tones of yellow and green, embroidered in tent st.

Cut corn: double yarn in tones of yellow, embroidered in satin st.

Hayfields and stubble: various light and medium greens used 4-fold in a wide satin st for the hayfield. The stubble is worked in double yarn in tent st.

Bushes: deep green yarns, shown as shaded patches in the diagram. Short lengths of yarn are made into pom-pons and sewn on to the fields after these have been stitched.

Stream and pond: two or three different blues used together, embroidered in chain st.

Bridge: knitted in simple rib and stitched over the stream joining the street across the water.

Fig 3: plan of the rug base

Trees

You will need two tubes of cardboard for the inside of the trees; the tops are made of large pom-pons in thick, green yarn. The trunk is knitted as follows: using dark brown yarn on No10/3¼mm needles, knit a piece measuring 5½in/14cm long. Roll this around the cardboard tube and sew it up lengthways. Glue the pom-pon to the top. Each tree will stand more firmly if it is given a base of either tufted canvas or cardboard.

Flowers and plants

These can be knitted, crocheted, or made of tiny tufts of yarn from small oddments. They are extremely simple and can be made without a pattern; just crochet chains and link them together at a central point. These are scattered here and there around the scene, in front of the cottages, and around the trees and bushes.

BUILDINGS

As these can be knitted with any kind of yarn, from a fine 3 ply to thick rug-thrums, no specific instructions have been given regarding needle sizes, stitches or rows. Instead, each knitter should consult the chart opposite and make the building pieces to those measurements. It will be noted that extra buildings appear on some photographs; these have been made from the same pattern. Each building is filled with a block of foam cut to the correct shape. This should be made

The farmer and his wife look out over their fields.

16

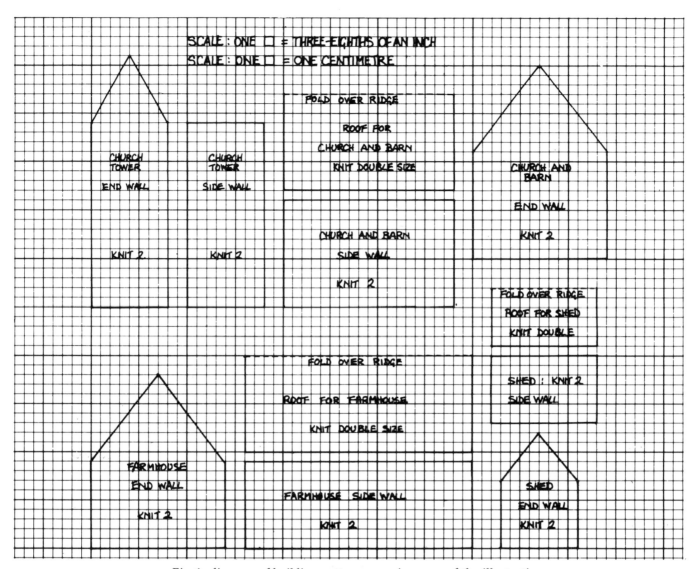

SCALE : ONE □ = THREE-EIGHTHS OF AN INCH
SCALE : ONE □ = ONE CENTIMETRE

FOLD OVER RIDGE

ROOF FOR
CHURCH AND BARN
KNIT DOUBLE SIZE

CHURCH
TOWER
END WALL

CHURCH
TOWER
SIDE WALL

CHURCH AND BARN
SIDE WALL

KNIT 2

CHURCH AND
BARN
END WALL
KNIT 2

KNIT 2.

KNIT 2

FOLD OVER RIDGE
ROOF FOR SHED
KNIT DOUBLE

FOLD OVER RIDGE

ROOF FOR FARMHOUSE

KNIT DOUBLE SIZE

SHED : KNIT 2
SIDE WALL

FARMHOUSE
END WALL
KNIT 2

FARMHOUSE SIDE WALL

KNIT 2

SHED
END WALL
KNIT 2

Fig 4: diagram of building patterns seen in many of the illustrations

slightly larger than the knitting to ensure a snug fit. Extra instructions for each building, and materials are given on this page.

Shed

This is the smallest of all the buildings, (see page 36). The walls are knitted in a k1, p2, rib pattern in brown, and the roof is worked in garter st in rust.

Barn

This pattern, (see page 36), is used also for the main part of the church, and for the stable building seen on page 29. The barn is made of dark-brown yarn with beige/rust for the roof, which is knitted in garter st. The walls are knitted in k1, p2 rib. The walls of the other buildings are of stocking st, with a ridge around the base of 6 rows of garter st.

The barn door is made in k1, p1 rib, decreasing at the top to make a curve. The edge is embroidered in chain st to give a crisp finish.

Church

White yarn is used for the main part, (see opposite), and rust-mottled tweed for the roof, with oddments of dark and mid-brown.

Farmhouse

Beige yarn is used for the walls, rust for the roof, and small amounts of other colours for windows and doors (see opposite). The roof is knitted in double rib (k2, p2 on every row) and the walls begin with 6 rows of garter st, before continuing in stocking st.

FIGURES

The materials required are:
6 pipe-cleaners for each figure
Wadding (about ½ yard/metre should be enough for all the figures and animals). Thick pink yarn for binding. Fine 3 ply skin-coloured yarn for knitted body-coverings. (A 1oz/25gm ball will be enough for all the adults and children.) One pair each No13/2¼ mm and No12/2¾ mm needles, crochet hooks, wool needles, scissors and tape-measure.

Basic body

The following instructions are for all the figures; the sizes for the children are given in Fig 9.

Take two pipe-cleaners and lay them end to end overlapping by about ¾ in/2 cm. Twist them together where they overlap, to make one long piece, (see Fig 5). Now do the same with two more, and lay the two pieces side by side. Bend into shape as shown, to make the head, (see Fig 6). Twist the legs gently together and turn the feet up very slightly to make the legs even. Take two more pipe-cleaners and lay them

evenly across the shoulders, twisting them as shown. Turn up the end slightly to shorten the arms, (see Fig 7).

Cover the head and body with a piece of padding, and bind this gently in place with the thick pink yarn, winding it also around the legs and arms to thicken them. Draw the yarn tightly around the neck to define it, (see Fig 8). The children are made in the same way as the adults except that the pipe-cleaner frame is shortened at the hands and feet.

KNITTED BODY COVERING

(Note. The farmer's wife is made differently, see page 23). The body-covering for the children is made in the same way as the adults, but you should check the length of each piece against the child's figure before finishing. You may also find that you need one or two less sts than the adult pattern. The little girl wears white ankle socks which should be knitted into the bottom of the legs before the shoes.

Use the No13/2¼ mm needles and the fine skin-coloured yarn. Begin with the main body piece which

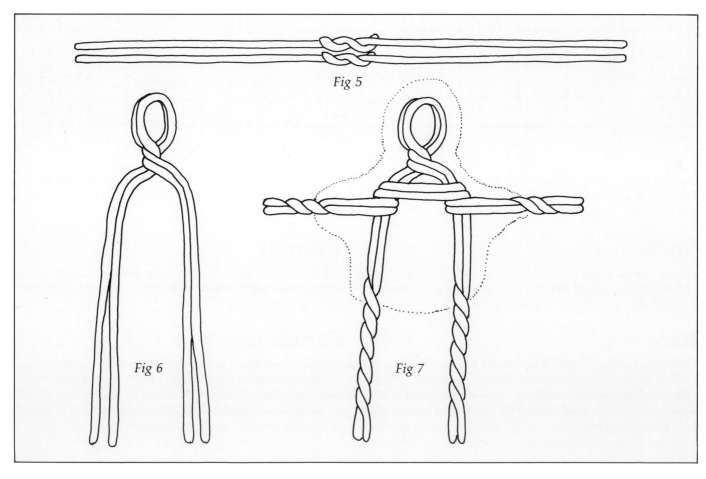

Fig 5

Fig 6

Fig 7

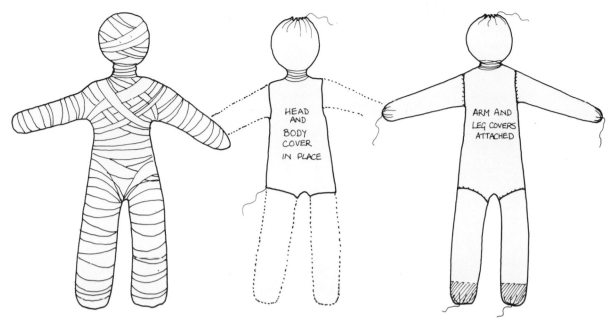

Fig 8: the figure wrapped and covered with the knitted pieces

also covers the head. Cast on 22sts and work in ss for 16 rows from the top of the legs to the under-arm. This should now be checked against the figure framework as sizes will vary depending on yarn, tension and the padding on the body. Now divide for the arms. K6. Turn and work on these 6sts alone for 6 more rows. Break off the yarn. Attach the yarn to the other group of sts and k10. Work on these 10sts alone for 6 more rows. Break off yarn. Attach the yarn to the last group and work 6 more rows, but do not break the yarn. Now continue across all the sts for 13 more rows. (Again, this should be checked against the figure, bearing in mind that the knitting will stretch a little.) Do not cast off; gather the sts on to a threaded wool needle and draw them together. Slip the arms into the holes, and the last sts on top of the head. Sew up the back seam, wrapping the yarn tightly around the neck. At the base, pull the two edges together in the centre between the legs, ready for the leg-pieces to be joined on, (see Fig 8).

Arms

Cast on 10sts and work 18 rows in ss. Check to see whether this piece fits the arms on your figure. K 2 tog all along the next row, then thread the yarn on to the last 5sts and gather up. Slip this on to the arm with the gathers at the hand end, and sew up. Attach the piece around the armhole, and make another piece to match.

Legs

Cast on 10sts and work in ss for the length of the leg as far as the ankle – about 22 rows. If the legs are not as long as you would like them to be, take this opportunity to add more rows at this point and pad the shoe area with wool before sewing up.

The last 6 rows are worked in shoe colour in either ss or gt s. They are finished off in the same way as the hands (the farmer wears separately made boots). Sew the cast-on edge to the bottom of the body covering around the top of the leg.

Make another in the same way, (see Fig 8).

Faces and hair

The hair and beards are embroidered using scraps of brown and fair wool, and the spectacles are made of brass wire. The features are also embroidered on using oddments of yarn.

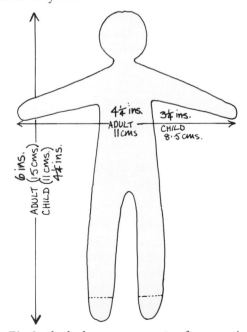

Fig 9: the body measurements after covering

19

The mother and father, two children and baby, and the dog.

Father

Use contrasting oddments of yarn and lots of colours to add interest to the figure.

TROUSERS

Knitted in gt s on size No13/2¼ mm needles in fine 3 ply or 4 ply. Cast on 22sts and knit 26 rows.
Row 27; cast off 12sts and k to end of row (10sts).
Row 28; k10, turn and cast on 12sts. K to end of row (22sts).
Knit across all sts for 25 more rows. Cast off.
Fold the two side edges towards each other and sew up the centre back seam. Now sew up the inside leg seams, (see Fig 10).

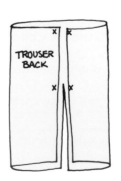

Fig 10: the trouser pattern

SHIRT

The back and front are worked in one piece, with separate sleeves (see above). Use size No12/2¾mm needles, cast on 12sts and work 16 rows in ss.

Next row; k3, cast off 6sts, k to end.

Next row; p3, turn and cast on 3sts, k back to the beg of the row, working into the back of the 4th st. Work 5 more rows on these 6sts ending on a p row. Break off yarn and attach it to the other 3sts, casting on 3 more sts at the same time on the neck edge.

Purl back to the end of the row, working into the back of the 4th st. Work 5 rows on these 6sts ending with a k row, then work across the other 6sts also, to join the two sides.

Next row; p. Work 8 more rows and cast off.

Sleeves

Cast on 15sts and work 2 rows in ss.

Cast off 2sts at beg of next 2 rows.

Next row; k 2 tog, k 7, k 2 tog, (9sts). Cast off p-wise. Make another one the same. Lay the shirt body section out flat and sew the sleeve, centrally positioned, to this. Then sew the underarm and side seams all at once. You may wish to work a row of crochet around the neck to finish it off. The back opening may be stitched up once it is on the figure but to make it easy to remove, you may prefer to attach a tiny button and loop.

RUCKSACK

The rucksack is shown on page 26. Using 3 ply yarn and No13/2¼mm needles, cast on 10sts and work in stocking st for 24 rows.

Dec one st at each end of the next 2 rows, then work 2 more rows. Cast off 6sts. The strap is a crochet chain, and the flap has an edge of crochet to keep it flat. It can be fastened with a press-stud.

Mother

The mother is wearing the same trousers as the father, so follow the pattern on page 20.

PULLOVER

This is made in one piece from one sleeve edge to the other. It opens down the back from neck to hem (see Fig 11).

Use No12/2¾mm needles and 3 ply or 4 ply yarn.

Cast on 16sts and work 12 rows in ss.

Cast on 8 more sts at beg of the next 2 rows, working into the back of the 9th st on each row (32sts). Work 4 more rows, then divide for the neck opening as follows:

K15, cast off 2sts, k to end of row.

Work 3 rows on these 15sts.

Next row; * k2, yarn forward, k 2 tog, * 3 times. K3. This makes 3 buttonholes.

Next row; p, then cast off.

Rejoin the yarn to the other sts and work 8 rows, beg with a p row.

Next row; cast on 17sts, p back across all 32sts, purling into the back of the 18th st.

Work 5 more rows, ending with a p row.

Cast off 8sts at beg of the next 2 rows, and work 12 rows in ss.

Next row; cast off.

Attach 3 tiny buttons to the back opening, and sew up the seams.

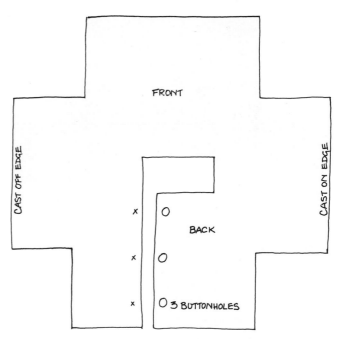

Fig 11: diagram of the farmer's shirt and the mother's pullover

The farmer and his donkey.

Farmer

The same shirt pattern is used as for the mother's pullover, though the colour is different. The trousers are also the same, except that the farmer's have crocheted straps, or braces. The farmer's hat may be knitted or crocheted: here is the knitted version.

HAT

Use 3 ply yarn and size No13/2¼ mm needles: cast on 22sts.
Work 4 rows in ss, then k 2 tog all along the row.
Purl the next row, then gather the rem sts on to a thread and leave. With the right side facing you, pick up 22sts from the cast-on edge and k back, inc into every st.
K 2 rows and then cast off. Sew up the back seam, and make a crochet chain to go around the brim.

BOOTS

Use No13/2¼ mm needles and dark-brown 3 ply yarn.
Cast on 15sts and work 10 rows in ss.
Row 11; p, then work in reversed ss for 6 more rows.
Next row; k 2 tog all along the row to the last st, k1.
Gather up the rem sts on to a length of yarn and sew up. Place a small amount of padding in the toe of the boot and fix on to the foot.

Farmer's wife

The farmer's wife wears a long skirt which is enclosed at the base with an oval-shaped piece of card, so her legs do not need a knitted covering. Unlike the other figures, her clothes are not removable; her dress-bodice and head-covering are made in one piece, as are the sleeves and hands.

BODICE AND HEAD-COVERING

Use size No13/2¼mm needles and dress-coloured yarn.

Cast on 22sts and work in ss for 4 rows. Then divide for the arms: k6, turn, and work on these 6sts for 6 more rows. Cut the yarn and attach it to the other group of sts.

K 10, turn and work on these 10 sts for 6 more rows. Complete as for first section.

Work 6 rows on the next 6sts, then p across all 22sts. Work 4 more rows to finish the neckline.

Change to the skin-coloured yarn, and work in ss for 11 rows. Finish the top of the head as for the other figures.

SLEEVES AND HANDS

These are worked in gt s and ss respectively.

Using dress-coloured yarn, cast on 10sts and k 16 rows.

The farmer's wife, watched by the kitten and the cockerel, picks lettuces.
The stables and trees are in the background.

The farmer's wife and her mule.

Change to skin-coloured yarn and ss. Work 4 more rows.

On the 5th row, k 2 tog 5 times.

Gather the rem sts on to a thread and sew the hand and arm seam on the wrong side. Reverse the sleeve and attach to the figure.

SKIRT

Use size No11/3 mm needles and dress-coloured yarn, cast on 25sts and work in gt s for 6¼ in/16 cm. Cast off and sew this edge to the cast-on edge. Gather one edge of the tube and attach it to the bodice. Cut an oval-shaped card for the base of the skirt and stick it in place inside the hem to give a firm base to the figure.

APRON

Use size No14/2 mm needles, pale yarn, cast on 14sts, work 4 rows gt s, then 22 rows ss. Cast off. Gather the top slightly and sew on to the figure. Crochet a long chain about 8in/20cm, and sew this around the waist-line to tie at the back.

HAIR

Cut 6 × 8¾ in/15 × 22 cm lengths of coppery-red yarn and sew these centrally to the middle of the head. Then tie them together at the nape of the neck, securing them there with a few sts. Tie them again further down and sew on to the middle of the head at the top, twisting them into a knot and sewing them down firmly. Embroider the features.

Children

The children's clothes can be knitted up using just a few oddments of brightly coloured yarn.

TROUSERS

These are worked as for the adults, (see pattern page 20), except that they are shorter. Use size No13/2¼ mm needles, cast on 12sts and, to divide for the legs, cast off half the stitches.

JUMPERS

The boy's jumper is knitted in stripes but the instructions are the same as for the father's shirt, except for the sleeves. Each piece should be measured for length against the figure. The girl's jumper is a sleeveless version of the same pattern.

Sleeve for boy's jumper
Cast on 12sts and work 2 rows in ss.
Cast off 2sts at beg of next 2 rows.
Next row; k 2 tog, k 4, k 2 tog, (6sts). Cast off p-wise.

HAIR

The hair of both children is embroidered on to the head in fair and dark yarns; the little girl may have plaits.

The children and their pony, not to mention the dog.

The family enjoys a picnic under the trees.

Baby

The same kind of wire construction is used as for the other figures, but on a much smaller scale. Only three pipe-cleaners are used for the frame, two for the head and body and one bent in half for the arms. Turn the feet and hands up so that the overall length is about 2⅜ in/6 cm and the width across the arms is about 1¾ in/4.5 cm. There is no need to use padding on this small frame, only thick pink yarn to bind it round. The body-covering and rompers are made in one piece in ss, beginning with the head.

KNITTED COVER AND ROMPERS
Use size No13/2¼ mm needles and fine pink yarn, cast on 12sts and work 8 rows. Change to blue yarn and work 2 rows. Now make holes for the arms as follows:

k2, yarn forward, k 2 tog, k 4, yarn forward, k 2 tog, k 2.
Work across all sts making a total of 10 blue rows, then divide for the legs.
K 6 and work on these 6sts for 10 rows. Change to pink yarn and work 4 rows. Leave the sts on a thread. Work the other leg to match. Slip the arms through the two holes and sew up the leg and back seams. Now make the two arms: cast on 6sts in white yarn and work 4 rows. Purl the next row, then change to pink yarn and work 2 rows. Draw the thread through the rem sts and complete as for other arm. Embroider features and a little hair if you wish.

ANIMALS

Begin with the simplest and smallest, and work towards the larger and more complicated animals.

Ducks

Cast on 22sts in white yarn and k 3 rows.
4th row; k 2 tog, k to end of row.
Repeat this row 11 more times.
Knit 9 more rows on the rem 10sts. Cast off.
Fold the shape as shown, stuff, and finish off with beak and eyes.

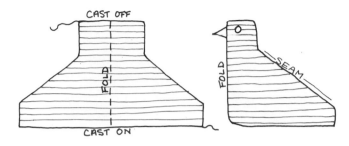

Fig 12: basic and sewn shape for the duck

The little boy and the ducks.

Some hens and a cockerel scratch around the barn.

Hens and cockerels

You will need small amounts of 3 ply or 4 ply yarn in brown, white and red, a very small amount of yellow for the beaks, some brightly coloured embroidery cottons for the cockerel's tail and for his legs. You will need half a pipe-cleaner plus wadding for the bodies. Use size No12/2¾ mm and No11/3 mm needles. All birds are knitted in gt s.

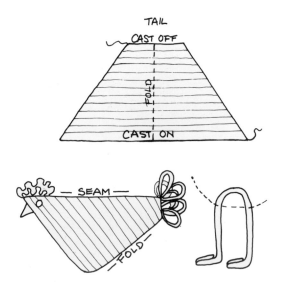

Fig 13: basic shape, sewn shape and legs for the hen

Cast on 18sts in brown yarn and k 3 rows.
4th row; k 2 tog, then k to end of row.
Repeat row 4 until there are only 6sts left. Cast off.
Complete as shown in the diagram, making a crochet chain for the tail feathers. The cockerel's tail is larger and more brightly coloured. Use the half pipe-cleaner to make the legs and wrap it round with yarn before stitching into place.

Kitten

The kitten is shown opposite and on page 23.
You will need small oddments of 3 ply or 4 ply yarns in grey, white and black, or any cat colour you wish. Size No12/2¾ mm or No11/3 mm needles. Cast on 8sts in body-colour and work in ss.
Knit 1 row.
2nd row; inc into every st (16sts), then work 8 rows.
Row 11; k 2 tog all along the row (8sts).
Work 6 rows then draw a thread through the sts, pad the shape and sew up. Gather a thread around the neck. Make a tail of 4sts and 10 rows in ss.

Legs
Use size No13/2¼ mm needles, cast on 7sts with white yarn and work 9 rows ss. Make 4.

Ears
Cast on 3sts with black yarn, k 2 rows and cast off. Make 2.

Pig

You will need small amounts of pink or beige yarn. Note that in this version shown below, the legs are made separately from the body. Begin at the back and work towards the nose, using gt s on size No12/2¾ mm or No11/3 mm needles.

Cast on 20sts and k 24 rows.

Now dec on alternate rows as follows:

Row 25; k 7, k 2 tog, k 2, k 2 tog, k 7.

Row 27; k 6, k 2 tog, k 2, k 2 tog, k 6.

Row 29; k 5 and continue in the same manner as above.

Row 31; k 4 ditto.

Work 2 rows straight.

Row 34; k 2 tog, to the end of the row.

Row 35; p and then draw the last sts on to a thread, using this to sew up the body after padding it.

Legs

Use size No14/2 mm needles, cast on 8sts, and work 10 rows ss. Cast off. Fold, pad and join to body. Make 4. Embroider the eyes and make a curly tail of crochet.

The farmer, his pigs and the kitten,
outside the barn on the right and the stable.

Some sheep grazing by the shed.

Sheep

For the body you will need white yarn (bouclé, or curly wool is best), and fawn or black yarn for the faces and legs. You will also need 2 pipe-cleaners for the legs. The body is knitted in gt s, and the faces and legs in ss. You will also need wadding, needle sizes No13/2¼ mm and No11/3 mm, and yarn for the eyes.

Body
Begin at the tail-end, using white yarn and No11/3 mm needles, cast on 18sts and k 17 rows.
Dec one st at the beg and the end of the next row, and also on row 20 and 22.

Row 23; change to No14/2 mm needles and fawn or black yarn and work 8 rows in ss (this is the nose). Draw the rem sts on to a length of yarn, pad the cavity and sew it up with the seam underneath.

Legs
Take 2 pipe-cleaners and fold them in half. Now curve them round and insert one end into one side of the body and out at the other, through the knitting where one pair of legs should be. Do the same for the other pair, then bend the wire up so that it is 4-fold and half

as long. The knitted leg covering can now be slipped over these and sewn in place.

Using size No13/2¼ mm needles and fawn or black yarn, cast on 8sts and work 10 rows. Draw up the sts at the foot, and make 3 more pieces the same.

Ears

With No14/2 mm needles, white yarn, cast on 3sts, and work 5 rows. Do not cast off. Draw sts up and sew on with rem thread. Make 2.

Dog

Instead of being crocheted, as in the photograph below, this version is knitted and the legs are made separately from the body. It will, however, look more or less the same as the one illustrated.

You will need small amounts of white 3 ply or 4 ply yarn, and tan for the spots and ears, 4 pipe-cleaners for the frame, padding and a thick yarn for binding. Also, size No13/2¼ mm needles.

Make the frame as shown in the diagram overleaf,

The farmer cuts hay and the boy rakes it up.
Their tools lean against the shed.

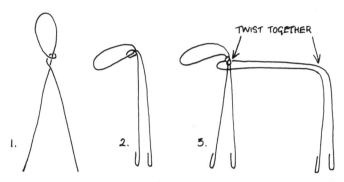

Fig 14: the wire framework for the dog

1.   2.   5.   TWIST TOGETHER

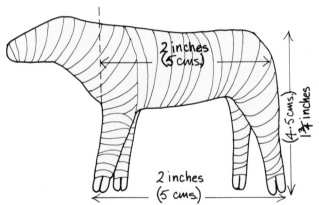

Fig 15: the dog after wrapping showing approximate measurements

2 inches (5 cms.)

2 inches (5 cms.)

(4-5 cms.) 1¾ inches

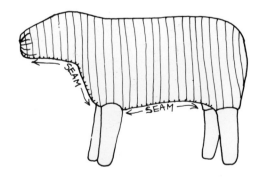

Fig 16: the dog with body cover in place

SEAM

SEAM

noting that each piece of wire is a *double* pipe-cleaner. Pad it lightly and bind this in place ready for the knitted cover (see Fig 15).

Begin at the nose, and cast on 12sts.
Rows 1–6; ss.
Rows 7–12; gt s.
Inc one st at beg of the next 6 rows (18sts).
K 6 rows straight.
Inc one st at beg of next 2 rows (20sts).
K 16 rows straight.
Last row; k 2 tog to end of row, thread the length of yarn on to a needle and draw this through the 10sts. This is the dog's tail-end. Gather the cast-on edge on to the dog's nose and sew up as in the diagram (Fig 16).

Legs
Cast on 6sts, k 12 rows. Gather last sts on to a thread for the foot-end. Pad and draw up; attach to body. Make 4.

Ears
In brown or tan yarn, cast on 4sts, k 4 rows.
Last row; k 2 tog twice, then cast off. Make 2.

Cow

This is worked in gt s all through, except for the horns and the udder. In this version, the legs are made separately from the body. You will need small amounts of 3 ply or 4 ply yarn in beige, or any other cow-colour you choose, also oddments of pink and brown. Size No13/2¼ mm and No11/3 mm needles and padding.
It will be found more convenient to attach the udder *before* the legs!
With size No11/3 mm needles, cast on 30sts and begin at the tail-end of the body. K 38 rows.
Row 39; k 2 tog, k 6, k 2 tog, k 10, k 2 tog, k 6, k 2 tog, (26sts).
Row 40; knit.
Row 41; dec one st at each end of row.
Repeat the last 2 rows until there are 18sts on the needle.
Row 48; k 12, turn and k 6. Work on the centre sts only – turn and k 5.
Turn and k 4.
Turn and k 2.
Turn and k 4.
Turn and k 6.
Turn and k to the end of the row.
Next row; dec one st at both ends of the row (16sts).
K 10 more rows.
Last row; k 2 tog to the end of the row, and gather these 8sts on to a thread and draw up.
Pad and close up the body.

The farmer tends his cows and the hens look for seeds.

Legs

Using size No13/2¼mm needles, cast on 12sts and work in gt s for 22 rows. Gather these sts on to a thread and draw up to form the foot, then sew up the seam, pad firmly and attach the cast-on edge to the body. Make 3 more in the same way. *Note:* the legs will look different from those in the photograph.

Ears

No13/2¼mm needles, cast on 5sts, work 8 rows of gt s.
Row 9; k 2 tog, k 1, k 2 tog.
Row 10; k 2 tog, k 1. Cast off. Fold in half and attach to the head as shown in the picture. Make 2.

Horns

Use paler yarn and No13/2¼mm needles, working in ss.
Cast on 6sts, work 10 rows, then k 2 tog 3 times.

Draw the 3 sts on to a thread and sew up. Pad slightly and attach as shown. Make 2.

Udder

Pink 3 ply yarn, No13/2¼mm needles, work in ss. 16sts, 6 rows.
Gather all sts on to a thread and draw up, pad and sew on.
Make 4 teats: 4sts, 4 rows of ss. Draw sts on to thread and sew on.

Tail

Using double yarn, make a crochet chain 2 in/5 cm long, and sew a tassel to the end. Fix this high up on the cow's back.
Embroider the markings on to the cow's body and the eyes and nose on to its face.

The skewbald pony in a field of flowers.

Pony

This is knitted all in one piece like a skin, beginning with the back legs and ending with the nose (Fig 17). It is a little more complicated than any of the other patterns, so if you prefer a simpler version it is suggested that you use the cow (body and legs) pattern, and substitute the pony's ears, mane and tail. You will need 3 ply or 4 ply yarns for the main body-colour and small oddments for the mane and tail. Padding will also be needed as well as needles size

No13/2¼ mm and No11/3 mm, and an extra pair. Garter st is used for all except the nose, and the hooves are made separately.

With the No11/3 mm needles, cast on 46 sts and k 5 rows.

Next row; k 22, inc into next 2 sts, k 22 (48 sts).

Knit 7 more rows.

Row 14; k 23, inc into next 2 sts, k 23 (50 sts).

Row 15; k 8, turn and k 5 rows on these 8 sts with an

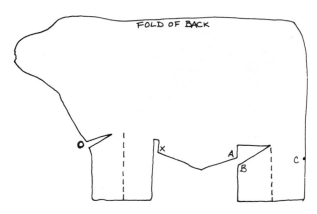

Fig 17: the shape of the pony skin

extra needle. Cast these 8 sts off and break off the yarn.

Rejoin the yarn to the centre section and k to the end of the row.

Row 17 as row 15.

Row 18; rejoin yarn to centre section and knit to end of row. Knit 3 rows on these 34sts

Row 22; cast on 3 sts, and k to end of row (37 sts).

Row 23; cast on 3 sts, and k to end of row (40 sts).

Row 24; inc into first st, k 18, k 2 tog, k 18, inc into last st (41 sts). Knit 7 more rows.

Row 32; k 2 tog, k 18, k 2 tog, k 17, k 2 tog (38 sts). Knit 6 more rows.

Rows 39 and 40; cast off 3 sts at beg of these 2 rows (32sts).

Rows 41 and 42; cast on 8 sts and k to end of row (48 sts).

Knit 10 rows on these 48 sts.

Row 53; k 8, turn and work 5 more rows on these 8 sts. Cast off.

Rejoin yarn to the centre section and k to end.

Row 55; as row 53. 32 sts remain.

Rejoin yarn to centre section, cast on 3 sts and k to end.

Row 57; cast on 3 sts and k to end (38 sts).

Shape neck

Next row; k 7, turn and k back on these 7 sts.

Next row; knit across all sts.

Repeat the last instructions 3 more times (i.e. twice at each side), then shape the top of the head.

Next row; k 23, turn, k 8, k to end.

Next row; knit across all sts.

Repeat this procedure twice more.

Shape nose

Next row; k 2 tog all along the row.

Now work 10 rows in ss.

Next row; k 1, k 2 tog all along the row, and gather the last sts on to a thread.

Ears

Use size No13/2¼ mm needles and work in ss. Cast on 7sts and work 5 rows. Then dec one st at each end of the 6th and 8th rows.

Draw the rem 3sts on to a thread and gather up. Make 2.

Hooves

Cast on 12sts in black yarn, and work 4 rows in gt s, then draw up all sts on to yarn and sew up to make a cup shape. Make 4.

Sew these on to the bottom of each leg.

Sew eyes and nostrils as shown, and cut lengths of contrasting yarn for the mane and tail.

Making up

Run a gathering thread around the cast-on-edge, then gather up to make a rounded tail-end. The padding of the 'pony-skin' is important to the success of the overall shape as it will tend to look very strange until the end of the process, when its eyes, ears, hooves mane and tail, have been added.

The diagram shows how to sew up the skin. Pad the legs before the body, and manipulate the padding gently to get a good shape, especially in the body around the neck.

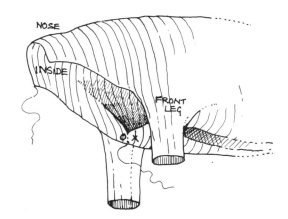

Fig 18: the front part of the pony showing the method of sewing the legs and under-seam

Donkey and mule

The basic shape is the same as that of the pony, but the donkey's mane and tail are different. See the photographs on pages 22 and 24. Also their ears are longer.

Rabbit

I have left the simplest one until last. It is made of a large white pom-pon body with two long knitted (or crocheted) ears. Tie a length of wool tightly around one side of the pom-pon to create the rabbit's head, then attach the ears.

The two children play with their rabbit.

ENCHANTED CASTLE

*The enchanted folk and animals
play happily beneath the castle walls,
while the brave knight
guards the little kingdom.*

CASTLE

This is the enchanted castle where the handsome prince lives with his brave knights. The exact height depends on the materials you have available, so the instructions given here are only general ones to illustrate how this model was made. It could easily become the container for all the small characters in this chapter, and would be a good project for a group of people to make.

You will need odd balls of grey and green DK yarn to cover the walls etc, and oddments of brown, orange and black yarns for the roof and details.
No10/3¼ mm, No9/3¾ mm and No8/4 mm needles.
You will also need pliable card for castle walls and roofs, and thick card for the bases. A large sheet of the former will be needed, as the walls are double thick-

*The talking trees from the magic forest look on while
the wicked witch sweeps the battlements with her broomstick.*

ness, and the bases can be cut out of cardboard boxes. Toilet and kitchen roll tubes for turrets and towers. Glue and staples. Thick tapestry needles (for sewing), scissors, craft knife and pins.

Cardboard shape

For the base, draw round a dinner plate and cut 2 or 3 circles from 'box-card'. For the walls (see Fig 19), decide on the height of the tower and cut 2 strips of card to encircle the base, minus a gap of about 4 in/ 10 cm for the gateway. For extra strength, cut another piece to be stuck round the outside of the tower after the base and inside wall have been assembled. Fig 19 explains how these should be put together. Another narrow strip should be cut from spare card to go round the top edge as shown. Stick this in place and strengthen with staples too.

Cut two tall towers to go at each side of the gateway and make six small turrets as shown in Fig 19. Do not stick these in position yet.

Gateway towers

Use a fairly thick DK yarn and size No8/4 mm needles. Cast on 26sts and k 24 rows of gt s then change to ss and make reverse side the RS. Work 25 rows in rev ss. Begin the window: with RS facing, p 8, (k 1, p 1) for 10sts, p 8.
Next row; (WS) k 8, (p 1, k 1), for 10sts, k 8.
Next row; (RS) p 8, k 1, p 1, join in black yarn, k 6 in black, weaving in grey behind these 6 sts then in grey – k 1, p 1, p 8.
Next row; (WS) k 8, p 1, k 1, change to black p 6, change to grey, p 1, k 1, k 8.
Work these last 2 rows 5 more times (12 rows of window) the dec one black st at each side on every 2 rows, leaving off the moss st edges. Work 12 rows plain then make a set of small windows above as follows:
Next row; (RS) p 6, 2 black (4 grey, k 2 black) to last 6sts, p 6 grey.
Next row; k 6 grey, (p 2 black, k 4 grey) to last 8sts, k 2 black, k 6 grey.
Work 6 of these rows in all then change to grey to continue as before.
[Note: on the RS, on the first complete grey row above the windows, work 2 *knit* sts above the black sts of the previous row to avoid the colour change showing on the right side.]
Work 6 straight rows, then 10 rows of double moss st. Cast off in rib.
Sew up the 2 long sides and slip this on to the cardboard tube. Stick with glue at the top and bottom edges. Make 2.

Turrets

Using the same needles and yarn, cast on 24 sts and work in rev ss for 2 in/5 cm – about 14 rows – ending on a RS row (i.e. the rough side).
Cast on 2 sts and slide this piece on to the knob end of the needle. On the same needle, cast on another 12sts and work the same number of rows as the first piece. Push the two pieces together on the LH needle and work across both sets of sts, knitting through the back of the 2 cast-on sts and also on the next st. As you knit these 2 pieces together, weave the broken yarn in behind the knitting; this will not show on the RS. Work across these 26sts for 4 rows.
Now begin the windows as folls: break off 2 lengths of black yarn, each about 22 in/56 cm long and use these for the 2 separate windows to avoid tangling.
With WS facing (the smooth side) work as follows:
1st row; k 5 grey, y fwd, p 3 black, k 10 grey, y fwd, p 3 black, k 5 grey.
2nd row; p 5 grey, yarn to back and twist round black yarn, k 3 black, p 10 grey, yarn to back and twist round black yarn, k 3 black, p 5 grey.
Work 6 of these rows in all, remembering to twist the grey and black yarns at the beg of the 3 black sts to avoid making a hole.
Now work across all the sts in grey, but purl the 3sts above the windows (i.e. the black sts of the previous row) on the *first* row.
Work 4 grey rows and then cast off.
Sew up the edges from the top to within 2 in/5 cm of the lower edge, leaving the rest open to correspond with the slit in the centre of the knitting. Slip this on to the card tube, and align the 2 slits, then glue the knitting carefully in position so that no card shows. Glue round the top edge too. Make 6.

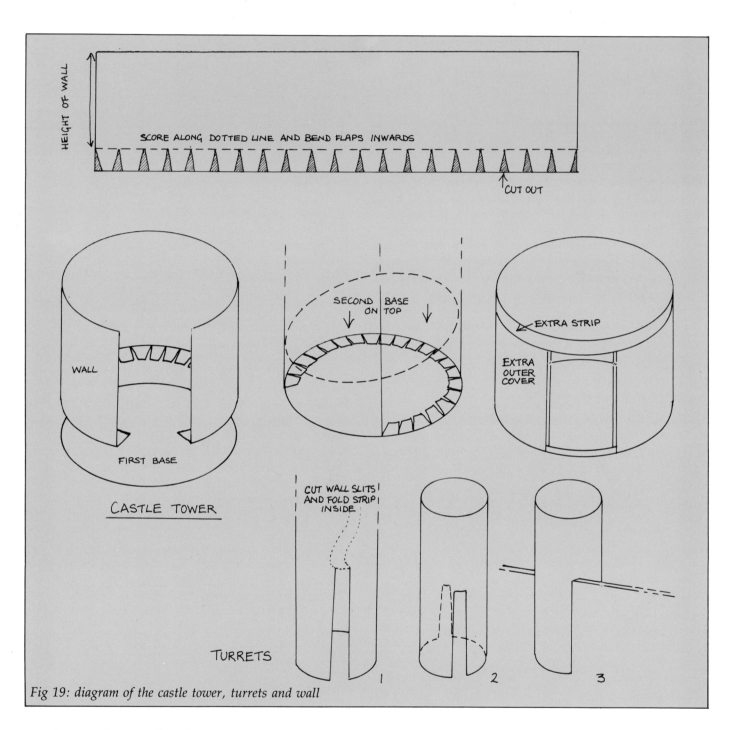

Fig 19: diagram of the castle tower, turrets and wall

The image contains the following labels:

HEIGHT OF WALL

SCORE ALONG DOTTED LINE AND BEND FLAPS INWARDS

CUT OUT

SECOND BASE ON TOP

EXTRA STRIP

EXTRA OUTER COVER

WALL

FIRST BASE

CASTLE TOWER

CUT WALL SLITS AND FOLD STRIP INSIDE

TURRETS

1   2   3

Pointed roofs for towers and turrets

Make the 2 card roofs, (see Fig 20). Although they are slightly different, the same knitted cover is used for both sizes as it stretches to fit. Oddments of orange and brown 3–4 ply yarns are used and pieces of bendy card, staples and glue. Size No9/3½ or No10/3¼ mm needles. Changes in yarn and needle sizes will produce roofs of a different size too. You may also need a crochet hook.

Cast on 40sts and work 2 rows in ss.
Row 3; (k 2 tog, k 8) 4 times, (36sts).
Work three straight rows between each decrease row.
Row 7; (k 2 tog, k 7) 4 times, (32sts).
Row 11; (k 2 tog, k 6) 4 times, (28sts).
Row 15; (k 2 tog, k 2) 7 times, (21sts).
Row 19; (k 2 tog, k 1) 7 times, (14sts).
Row 23; (k 2 tog) 7 times.
Next row; p 7. Break off yarn, leaving a long end.
Gather the last sts on to the length of yarn and sew up to fit the card shape.

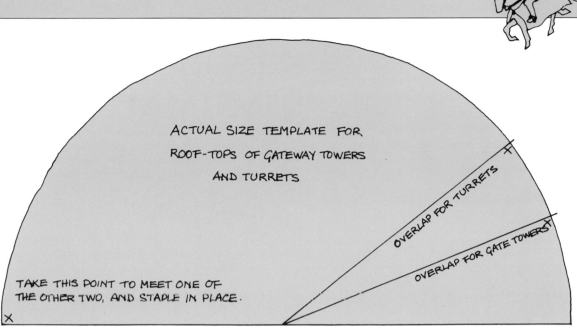

ACTUAL SIZE TEMPLATE FOR
ROOF-TOPS OF GATEWAY TOWERS
AND TURRETS

OVERLAP FOR TURRETS

OVERLAP FOR GATE TOWERS

TAKE THIS POINT TO MEET ONE OF
THE OTHER TWO, AND STAPLE IN PLACE.

Fig 20: diagram of the crenellations and roof tops of the gateway towers and turrets

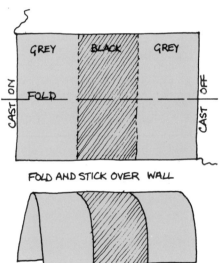

GREY BLACK GREY

CAST ON   FOLD   CAST OFF

FOLD AND STICK OVER WALL

To neaten the edge, a tiny crochet st has been worked in to each knit st of the cast-on edge using a size No11/3 mm hook and a simple dc st, but this is optional. On the 2 gateway towers, another row of chained loops has been worked for extra decoration, but this is also optional.

Walls

To suit all measurements and shapes, and to make the knitting both easier and more interesting, the walls have been designed in separate strips going from top to bottom. These are then sewn together into one long piece, and the length can then be determined by the size of the tower you have made. If several people are working on this project, this would be an easy and painless way of covering a large surface, as long as the length of each piece (i.e. from the top of the wall to the base) was reasonably accurate. Any pieces which are a little too long can be folded over the top, and the width is not critical. The various textures/knitting stitches used will make the wall more interesting, even cables and lace patterns would be fun when combined with plain pieces. It could even be used as a sampler!

The pieces used on this castle are between 20 and 30sts wide, using DK yarn on No8/4 mm needles, but there is no reason why different yarns cannot be used for this as long as the thicknesses are fairly similar. Use mossy green to suggest foliage too.

Crenellations

These are optional but add an authentic touch to the top of the castle walls, and are added as a series of long narrow strips after the walls have been covered with knitting and the turrets stuck in place on top of them. For the strip over the gateway, knit a narrow strip in rev ss to stretch from one gateway tower to the other – about 8–10sts wide, with 10 rows in grey, 10 in black and 10 more in grey. The exact measurements will depend upon the individual castles. The small strips between the turrets are made separately (see Fig 20) and are glued on top of the knitted walls as shown.

Drawbridge

This is simply an oblong of card sandwiched between 2 pieces of knitting, one side in brown (any ridged pattern works well) and the other a paler colour/tone in smooth ss. The size of the card should be large enough to fit closely inside the gate area between the 2 towers, and the bottom edge can be sewn to the edge of the base. Measure the width of your gateway and be sure to cast on enough sts to cover the card piece. This drawbridge needed 32sts for a piece of card 5 in/13 cm wide, and a fancy rib st was used as follows.

Large eyelet rib

(you need a multiple of 6sts + 2 extra).
RS row 1; * p 2, k 4, * rep to last 2sts, p 2.
WS row 2; k 2, * p 4, k 2 *, rep from * to end.
Row 3; * p 2, k 2 tog, y fwd twice, sl 1, k 1, psso, * to last 2sts, p 2.
Row 4; k 2, * p 1, k into first y fwd and p into 2nd y fwd, p 1, k 2, rep from * to end.

Order of assembly

1. Stick knitted strip over gateway.
2. Cover walls, stick along top and bottom edges. Leave a narrow strip of card showing down each edge of the gateway.
3. Cover turrets and position on walls at equal distances.
4. With a fine skewer or thick needle, punch holes at ¼ in/1 cm intervals all the way down the bare strip of card at the sides of the gateway.
5. Cover the 2 gateway towers and sew these firmly in position through their knitted covers and into the holes of the card at each side of the gateway. Use a strong double thread (of yarn) for this, and a long needle.
6. If necessary, knit a strip to cover the *inside* of the narrow strip of card above the gateway.
7. Make the card roofs and knitted covers and stick these in place by gluing the top edges of the *towers*.
8. Make the crenellation strips to cover the top edges of the walls and stick these in place.
9. Make the drawbridge card and knitting, and fix in place.
10. For extra effect, you may wish to line the inside of the castle too, or even make a lid for it.

FIGURES AND ANIMALS

The basic framework for most of the enchanted characters is simple to make (see Fig 21). 3 ply yarn is used for all the clothes.

Basic body

1. Two pipe-cleaners are laid together and twisted as shown to make the head and arms.

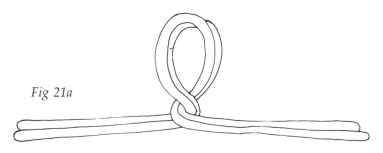

Fig 21a

2. Loop another pc, slip it over the head and twist it to make the top of the legs and body.

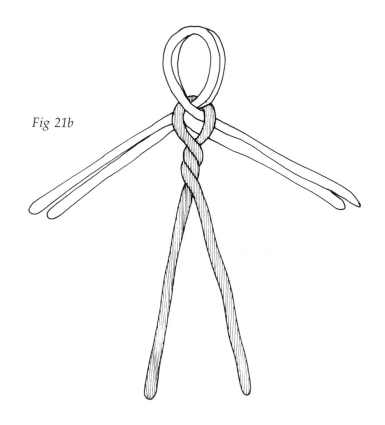

Fig 21b

Fig 21: making the wire frame body

3. Loop another pc in half and slip it over the head on the other side so that one loop lies to the front and the other to the back. Twist these and also the tops of the legs. Do a bit of pulling and tugging at this stage to ensure that the arms do not get pushed too far down the frame and look as if they come from the middle of the body.

Fig 21c

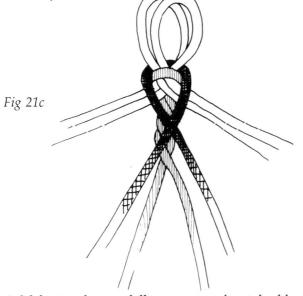

4. Make two legs as follows: one pc bent double, bend up about ½ in/1 cm at the folded end to form the foot. Lay this leg-section alongside the leg which is attached to the body, so that the overall height measures no more than 4½ in/11 cm. Bind the 2 leg pieces together with sticky tape. Turn up the arms to make them equal length.

Fig 21d

FIRST TWIST
THEN BIND
WITH
STICKY-
TAPE

TWIST
TOGETHER

5. Bind the head, body and arms with thick pink yarn, sewing the ends into the body and wrapping around the neck tightly as shown.

Fig 22a

Fig 22b

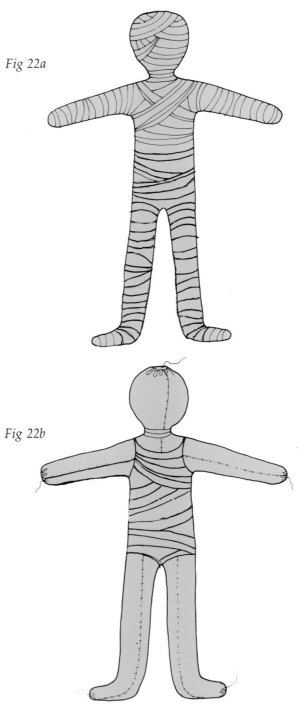

Fig 22: wrapping the body and the knitted covering

KNITTED BODY COVERING

Begin with the head and knit in ss throughout. Use 2 ply baby yarn and size No15/1½ mm needles, or finer. You will need about 20sts for the head covering, and about 18 rows to make a piece which continues down past the neck and well on to the shoulders. Gather the last sts on to a thread and draw these up to form the top of the head as shown. Sew the seam up the back and run a tight gathering thread around the neck. Sew the cast-on edge to the shoulder area.

Legs

Make legs on about 10sts as long as necessary for each figure to the top of the leg. Draw the last sts up on to a length of yarn and gather. Sew up the seam, and sew on to the complete body.

Arms

For the arms, you will need about 10sts. As with the legs, the pieces are not cast off but gathered up at the ends of the limbs. Attach the arm pieces well up on to the shoulder covering.

Prince

The handsome and charming prince of all the best stories wears eighteenth-century style dress, tight breeches tucked into tall riding boots, a fitted jacket edged with gold, the lace cuffs and cravat show at wrists and neck, and on his natural brown curls, (tied back with ribbon), he wears a three-cornered hat from which hangs a plume of feathers. The shirt, to make less bulk under the jacket, takes the form of a vest-front, so the lace cuffs are added to the sleeves of his jacket.

BREECHES AND BOOTS

These are made all in one piece. Beginning at the waist and using 3 ply deep yellow yarn and No14/2mm needles, cast on 10sts and work in ss for 25 rows. On the next row, dec one st at each end to make 8sts. Change to brown 3 ply for boots, and continue in ss for 18 rows, or until long enough to reach the end of the foot. Draw the sts up on to a threaded needle and sew up as far as the top of the boot. Make another piece the same. Sew centre back and centre front seams, slip on to the body, putting the feet into the boots, and sew down the legs. The boots may have a gold band embroidered round the tops. Darn all ends in.

SHIRT FRONT AND CRAVAT

This is simply an oblong of ss. Cast on 10sts and work 13 rows using fine white 3 ply. On the 14th row; knit. 15th row; purl. 16th row; knit, then cast off p-wise. These last rows form the neck edge. Sew this piece to the front of the body to slightly overlap the top of the breeches.

For the cravat, make 2 separate pieces and sew the narrow edges to the neckband of the shirt. Cast on 8sts and work in single rib for 5 rows.
Next row; (k 2 tog) 4 times.
Next row; k.
Next row; p, then cast off k-wise.
The second piece is the same except that the last 2 rows are omitted. This piece is sewn on top of the other.

COAT

Begin at the lower edge, and with No 14/2mm needles and deep yellow 3 ply yarn, cast on 22sts and work in single rib for 10 rows.
Next row; (k 2 tog, k 8) twice, k 2 tog.
Next row; p.
Next row; k 2 tog, k 6, k 2 tog, k 7, k 2 tog, (16sts).
Next row; p.
Continue in ss until the underarm division for the sleeves, (i.e. about 4 more rows).
Next row; work on the first 4sts for 7 rows.
Break off yarn and rejoin it to the centre 8sts. Work 7 rows. Break yarn and rejoin to the last 4sts and work 7 rows, then p across all 16sts. P one more row, k the next and cast off p-wise.
With gold metallic yarn, work an edge of crochet, using a No12/2.50mm crochet hook, all the way round the coat beginning at the centre of the back edge.

Sleeves

Cast on 10sts and work 8 rows in ss.
9th row; p, then break off yarn and change to white (as for shirt).
10th row; p, and cast off p-wise.
This makes a tiny white cuff on to which the lace ruffle is crocheted, so do not break the yarn, but using a No12/2.50 mm hook, crochet a frill along this edge as follows:
Next row; *3 ch, 1 dc into next ch sp * to end.

You may knit this frill if you prefer
Darn in unwanted ends at this stage and sew the lace cuff with rem white yarn. Sew up the rest of the sleeve and slide it on to the arm, placing the seam at the back. With metallic yarn, embroider a whip stitch over the p row along the cuff edge. Sew the sleeve to the coat armhole. Make 2.

HAIR AND FACE

Using mottled brown yarn and the same needles, cast on 14sts and work in gt s for 10 rows. Over the next 4 rows, k 2 tog at each end to make 6sts, (i.e. on alt rows).
Work in single rib for 8 rows on these 6sts, then cast off in rib. Gather the cast-on edge with a running st and sew up to form the crown of the head. Embroider the face, and then sew the hair on to the head. Make a

The handsome prince carries the princess away
on his white horse and they live happily ever after.

ribbon of crochet chain and tie this round the bunch of hair at the nape of the neck.

THREE-CORNERED HAT

For the crown of the hat, cast on 14sts and work 4 rows ss. Gather the last row and sew up the seam.
For the brim, cast on 16sts and work 2 rows in ss then *k 1, inc in next st, repeat from * to the end of the row, (24sts).
Next row; p.
Next row; * k 1, inc in next st, repeat from * to the end of the row, (36sts).
Next row; p.
Last row; k, then cast off p-wise and sew up the 2 short edges.
Sew the cast-on edge of the brim to cast-on edge of the crown, then fold up the brim to make 3 points at equal distances. Sew to the crown in the centre of each side (do not sew right along to the point, but run the needle through the crown to the centre of each side) with a few firm sts. Sew the hat to the head with one point at the front. The feathers are made from a crochet chain about 4 in/10 cm long, sewn into a bunch. Fluffy yarn is best for this.

Princess

The princess can be made to match your own individual ideas of what an enchanting princess should look like, colour of hair, clothes, and so on. Our princess wears a circlet of (crochet chain) glittery yarn over her auburn shoulder length hair, a deep blue embroidered gown (actually the pattern is knitted in) over an underskirt of white lace. The frilly white collar and sleeves ruffles, and the sparkling slippers complete the outfit, (see page 45).
You will need size No13/2¼ mm needles and a No12/2.50 mm crochet hook; 3 ply blue and white, a glittery yarn for the circlet, and a blue metallic yarn for the skirt pattern, and slippers. Brown (auburn) yarn for hair and oddments for features.

SKIRT

If the underskirt appears to be too 'holey' you may have to make another white layer beneath as I have done. This is simply an oblong gathered at the waist.

White underskirt and vest

The vest is a tiny oblong of rev ss, (8sts, 5 rows), sewn across the front of the body.
For the underskirt, cast on 50sts and work about 30 rows altogether, but to obtain the lacy effect, make half

of this amount in picot st or any other simple lacy st. (Picot st is made on 2 rows: * k 2 tog, y fwd repeat from * to end of row, then p the next row. This makes a row of holes).
The next-to-the-last row of the skirt should be decreased as follows; k 2 tog all across the row to make 25sts, then p the last row and cast off. Join the 2 side edges, gather the top, fit on to the waist, and sew in place.

Blue divided overskirt

Cast on 70sts in blue yarn (A) and use metallic blue yarn as the secondary colour (B). [Note: for a simpler version, use plain ss.]
Rows 1 & 2; use colour B and k 2 rows.
Row 3; A, (k 4, sl 2) to the last 4 sts, k 4.
Row 4; A, (p 4, sl 2 p-wise) to the last 4 sts, p 4.
Rows 5 & 6; as rows 3 & 4.
Rows 7 & 8; B, k all sts.
Row 9; A, k 1, (sl 2, k 4) to last 3 sts, sl 2, k 1.
Row 10; A, p 1, (sl 2 p-wise, P 4) to last 3 sts, sl 2, p 1.
Rows 11 & 12; as rows 9 & 10.
Repeat these 12 rows once more, then rows 1 & 2 again. Work 2 rows in A (ss).
Continue working in ss and dec on the k rows as follows:
Next row; (k 5, k 2 tog) 10 times.
Next and alt rows; p.
Next row; (k 2 tog, k 4) 10 times, (50sts).
Continue in ss on these sts until the waistline is reached, then k 2 tog all along the row (25 sts), then p one row. Cast off. Press the bottom edge *very gently* under a damp cloth to prevent it rolling up.

BODICE

Begin at the lower back (see Fig 23), cast on 9 sts and work in ss for 8 rows.

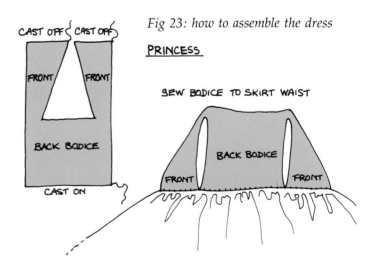

Fig 23: how to assemble the dress

PRINCESS

CAST OFF   CAST OFF

FRONT   FRONT

BACK BODICE

CAST ON

SEW BODICE TO SKIRT WAIST

BACK BODICE

FRONT   FRONT

SLIP THE BODICE AND SKIRT ON TO THE FIGURE AND STITCH THE TWO FRONT EDGES ONTO THE WHITE VEST.

9th row; k 2, cast off 5, k 2.

Work on the 2 sets of 2sts for 3 rows, then inc one st on the inside edge (i.e. the neck edge) on *alternate* rows until there are 5sts on each side. P one more row and cast off.

Making up

Gather the skirt waistband to fit the figure closely, leaving a gap of about ¼ in/6 mm at the front. Do not sew on to the figure at this stage. Now follow the instructions on the diagram.

Sleeves

With blue yarn, cast on 20sts and work in ss for 4 rows.

5th row; k 2 tog across all sts to make 10sts.

6th row; p.

Change to blue metallic yarn, k one row and cast off k-wise.

Sew up the side seam and gather the top edge to fit the armhole. Sew this in place on to the bodice, pushing the sleeve edge up on to the 'elbow'. Now make a lace cuff as follows: with the fine white yarn, cast on 24sts and k 2 rows, then k 2 tog across all sts to make 12. Cast off.

Gather the cast off edge, sew up the side edges, and then stitch the lace cuff to the sleeve edge. Make 2.

Lace collar

With the same yarn as the cuffs, cast on 40sts and k 2 rows. Picot st for 2 rows.

Next row; p 2 tog across all sts to make 20sts and cast off k-wise.

Sew cast-off edge to dress, (see Fig 23).

SHOES

Use blue metallic yarn, cast on 8sts and work in ss until long enough to slip over the foot (about 10 rows). Sew up the heel and gather the last row on to a thread and draw up over the toe. Sew this on to the foot.

HAIR AND FACE

Using brown (auburn) yarn for hair, cast on 16sts and work 4 rows in gt s.

5th row; p.

6th row; (k 2 tog, k 5) twice, k 2 tog, (13sts).

Work the next 13 rows in ss then gather all sts tog on a thread and draw up. Stitch this part to the top of the head, sew down the edges to the face and along the nape of the neck above the gt s edge.

Embroider the face.

The tiara, or circlet, is a crochet chain of glittery yarn made into a circle and stitched to the hair.

Knight

As the entire body is encased in shining armour, only the face requires a pink cover with embroidered eyes. For this, use a fine 2 ply dark flesh-coloured yarn on size No14/2 mm needles, and work on 22sts for 14 rows. Gather the last sts for the top of the head. The colour used on the cloak, shield and plume should all be the same, and if he rides on horseback, the trappings and harness should also be the same. The suit of armour is made from two main pieces; the helmet and tunic all-in-one, and the trousers and feet together. Any metallic colour will look good, gold, silver or bluish-silver. The helmet has another piece added on top of the 'hood' to give height, and this has a band of gold thread worked in. Measurements should be checked at all stages as yarns differ, see photo on page 48.

You will need size No14/2 mm and No15/1½ mm needles; metallic yarn, small amounts of contrasting coloured 3 ply for cloak, plume, and eyes; a small piece of thick card and one paper-stud for the shield. For the banner you will need a small lollipop stick and gold paper.

TROUSERS

These begin at the toe end. With metallic yarn and size No14/2 mm needles, cast on 10sts and work in ss for 24 rows, then inc one st at each end of next row (12sts). Work 25 more rows and cast off. Make another piece the same.

Sew these 2 pieces together from the top as far as the top of the legs, slip this part on to the body and pin at the waist. Gather the 2 cast-on edges at the feet, and sew up the leg seams (with the legs inside). Stitch the waist edge to the body.

TUNIC AND UNDER-HELMET

These begin at the lower edge of the front. Use the same yarn and needles, and * cast on 14sts and work 2 rows in ss. Work 2 rows of gold thread, then change back to silver for 2 rows. Dec one st at each end of the next row * and work 21 more rows, without shaping. (12sts.)

For the face-opening, k 3, cast off 6, k 3.

Work on the first set of 3 sts for 7 rows in ss, break the yarn and connect to the other 3 sts and work 6 rows on these.

Next row; turn, cast on 5sts, k across the other 3sts, (11sts).

Next row; p across the complete row, working into the back of the 9th st. Work 2 more rows, gather sts on to a thread and draw up.

For the back, work as for the front from * to *, then work 36 more rows, without shaping. Gather sts on to

The brave knight in silver armour and his horse are ready for battle.

a thread and draw up. Sew these 2 pieces tog from the lower edges, leaving a space for the arms. Slip this on to the body, sew the shoulders and round the neck and on up to the under-helmet. Sew the face-opening round the face.

Sleeve and hand

This is made all in one piece.

Cast on 20sts and work 22 rows in ss.

Do not cast off, gather the sts on to a thread and fit this part on to the hands. Stitch up the sleeve seam and attach the tops to the armhole of the tunic. Make another in the same way.

HELMET

The extra helmet fits over the top of the other and pulls well down over the forehead. Cast on 22sts and work in gt s for 7 rows, the 3rd and 4th of these being in gold thread.

8th row; p.

Gather all sts on to a thread and sew up the sides.

The plume is a thick, short tassel in the colours chosen for the other accessories. Sew it firmly to the top of the helmet and use a dab of glue to hold it in place at the back.

CLOAK

Gold 3 ply yarn was used for this but any other yarn will do as long as the measurements are checked against the figure. Using No15/1½ mm needles, cast on 12 sts and work 20 rows in ss. At this point, introduce bands of colour (6 rows were used on the model) and on the last of these rows, 3 extra sts were made, one at each end and one in the centre (15sts). Work 4 more rows and cast off. Sew the top edge round the neck.

SHIELD

This is a tiny shaped piece of gold card on to which has been glued a crocheted circle of gold yarn. It is fastened to the knight's left arm with a paper stud which passes through the centre of the circle and curves round on to the arm behind.

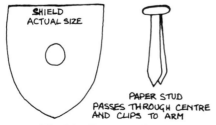

Fig 24: diagram of the shield

BANNER

Paint the lollipop stick silver. Cut a length of gold paper, fold and glue wrong sides together around the top of the pole, then cut out the banner shape.

Horse

It is quite important to spend time on the horse's framework, as this is the largest of our animals and must take the weight of a knight in full armour! (See page 50). Use plenty of pcs (allow 16 to 20), pad him carefully and wrap very firmly with yarn before making the cover. Remember that the cover adds something to the height and bulk of the horse. Aim for an upright stance, long slender legs and a not-too-fat body.

The padding should begin at the head-end: gently bandage the wire frame with long narrow strips of padding, making it bulkier around the shoulders, chest and hindquarters. Do not pad the legs except for the tops, but use the wrapping/binding yarn to separate the hindquarters under the tail. The legs should be wrapped with yarn to make them strong and smooth, but should remain slender.

The trappings worn during jousting were more for identification purposes than anything else as the colours and designs matched those of the rider, but for us, they serve the dual purpose of hiding a less-than-perfect model. They are, of course, optional, and can be made in any colour and design you choose. You may find that a row-counter would be useful.

You will need the following needles: No15/1½ mm, No13/2¼ mm, No12/2¾ mm and No11/3 mm, and a small crochet hook; 1oz/25 gm ball of 4 ply in main body-colour, small amounts for the mane and tail, and a bright colour for the trappings and harness and white yarn for the saddle (4 ply); blue and yellow 4 ply for the horse's coat; black yarn for the hooves; one gold or silver button to decorate the horse's coat.

KNITTED COVER

The forelegs and underbody gusset are made in 3 separate pieces; the back legs and body are made in 2 separate pieces which are then joined so that the head and neck are a continuation of these, (see Fig 26).

Forelegs

Use No12/2¾ mm needles and begin with black yarn for the hooves, cast on 8sts and work 4 rows in ss. Change to body colour and inc one st at both ends of next row, (10sts). Work 13 more rows, then inc again as before, and again on the 23rd row, (14sts).

P one more row and then cast off 2sts at beg of next 2 rows. Dec one st at both ends of next and every foll k row until only 2sts rem. Cast off. Make 2.

Sew the legs up and slip them on to the framework with the points to the outside and the seams inside.

Right back leg

* Cast on 8sts with black yarn and work 4 rows in ss.

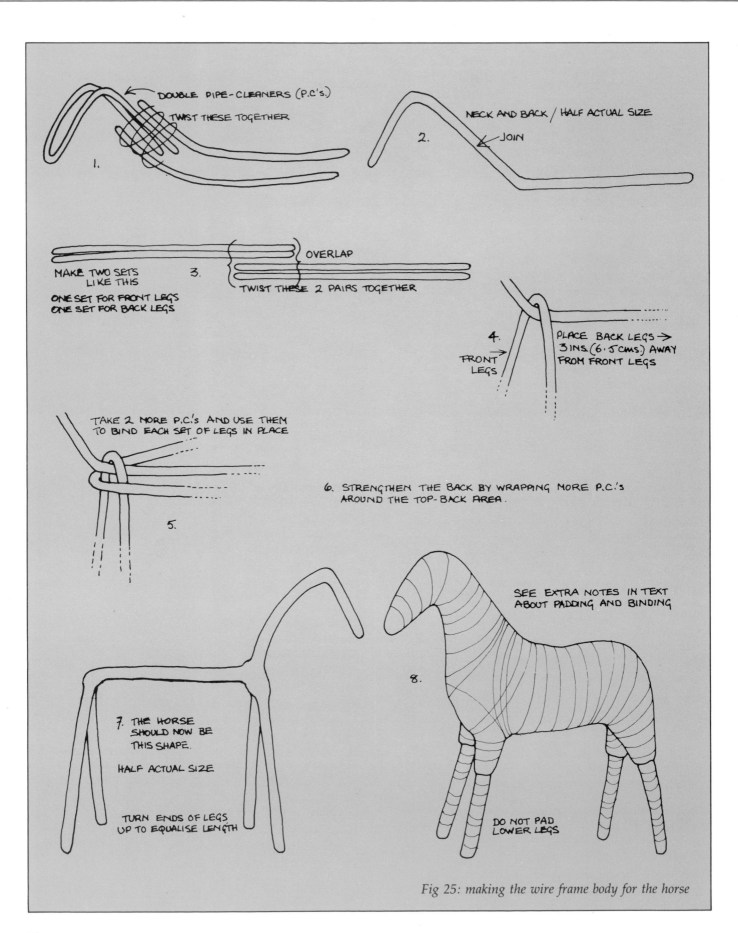

1. DOUBLE PIPE-CLEANERS (P.C.'s)
   TWIST THESE TOGETHER

2. NECK AND BACK / HALF ACTUAL SIZE
   JOIN

3. MAKE TWO SETS LIKE THIS
   OVERLAP
   TWIST THESE 2 PAIRS TOGETHER
   ONE SET FOR FRONT LEGS
   ONE SET FOR BACK LEGS

4. FRONT LEGS
   PLACE BACK LEGS 3 INS (6.5 CMS) AWAY FROM FRONT LEGS

5. TAKE 2 MORE P.C.'s AND USE THEM TO BIND EACH SET OF LEGS IN PLACE

6. STRENGTHEN THE BACK BY WRAPPING MORE P.C.'s AROUND THE TOP-BACK AREA.

7. THE HORSE SHOULD NOW BE THIS SHAPE.
   HALF ACTUAL SIZE
   TURN ENDS OF LEGS UP TO EQUALISE LENGTH

8. SEE EXTRA NOTES IN TEXT ABOUT PADDING AND BINDING
   DO NOT PAD LOWER LEGS

Fig 25: making the wire frame body for the horse

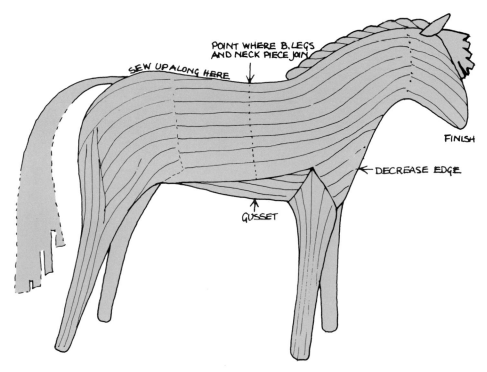

POINT WHERE B. LEGS
AND NECK PIECE JOIN

SEW UP ALONG HERE

FINISH

← DECREASE EDGE

GUSSET

Fig 26: assembling the knitted cover for the horse

Change to body-colour and inc one st at both ends of next row; (10sts).
Work 9 more rows (14 in all).
15th row; inc one st at each end of row, also on 19th, 21st and 23rd rows, (18sts). Purl alt rows.
25th row; inc in 1st st, k 8, M 1, k 8, inc in last st.
26th row; p.
27th row; inc, k 9, M 1, K 10, inc.
28th row; p, (24sts) *.
At this point, you can add extra rows to make the legs longer if you need to. You should have reached the top of the leg.
Next row; cast off 5sts, k to end.
Next row; cast off 3sts, p to end.
Next row; (k 3, inc in next st) 3 times, k 4.
Next row; p.
Next row; (k 4, inc in next st) 3 times, k 4.
Next row; p.
Next row; (k 5, inc) 3 times, k 4.
Next row; p.
Next row; (k 6, inc) 3 times, k 4, (28sts).
Begin shaping to turn on to the back:
Next row; p 2 tog, p across rest of sts until you reach the last st. Leave this on the LH needle, turn, and k back.
Repeat this procedure, leaving one extra st on the LH needle at the end of every p row (remembering to p 2 tog at the beginning) until 11sts rem unworked on the

LH side and 6 'worker' sts on the RH side, (17sts in all). Turn and k back, then p across all sts. Continue without shaping for 8 more rows.
Next row; k 12, turn and p back.
Next row; k 7, turn and p back.
Next row; k 2, turn and p back.
Work 2 complete rows across all these sts and then leave them on a spare needle until the left leg has been made.

Left back leg
Work as for right leg from * to *.
Next row; cast off 3 sts at beg of row, k to end.
Next row; cast off 5 sts at beg of row, p to end.
Next row; k 4 (inc in next st, k 3) 3 times. Purl alternate rows.
Next row; k 4 (inc, k 4) 3 times.
Next row; k 4 (inc, k 5) 3 times.
Next row; k 4 (inc, k 6) 3 times, (28sts).
Now begin the back shaping as follows:
Next row; k 2 tog, k to last st, leave this on LH needle, turn and p back.
Repeat these 2 rows, leaving one extra st on the LH needle at the end of every k row (remembering to k 2 tog at the beg) until 11sts rem unworked on the LH needle and 6 'workers' on the RH side, (17 sts in all). Turn and p back. Continue without shaping for 7 more rows.
Next row; p to last 2sts, turn and k back.

Next row; p to last 7sts, turn and k back.
Next row; p to last 12sts, turn and k back.
Work 3 complete rows leaving the sts on the needle.

Neck and head

Slip both sets of sts on to the same needle, back to back, and join them together by sewing (on the wrong side) along the back, from the needle to the 3 cast off sts. With the RS facing, cast on 10sts, k 2 tog on the centre 2 sts, k to end.

Next row; cast on 10sts and p to end.

Next row; k 2 tog, k to centre 2 sts and k these tog, k to last 2 sts, k 2 tog.

Next row; p.

Repeat the last 2 rows until there are 29sts.

Next row; k 2 tog at each end of row only.

Next row; p.

Repeat these last 2 rows once more, (25sts).

Next row; k 24, leave one st on LH needle, turn and p 23, leaving one st on LH needle. Turn, k to last 2sts, (leave 2 on LH needle) turn, p back to last 2 sts, and leave these on LH needle.

Continue in this way, leaving one extra st on LH needle at the end of every row until there are 8 unworked sts at each side of the row.

Turn and knit back on 17sts then p a complete row on 25sts.

Work 4 rows straight, then dec one st at each end of next row and continue without shaping on 23sts for 5 more rows.

Next row; k 2 tog, k 8, sl 1, k 2 tog, psso, k 8, k 2 tog.

Next row; p 19.

Next row; k 2 tog, k 15, k 2 tog.

Next row; p 17.

Next row; k 2 tog, k 5, sl 1, k 2 tog, psso, k 5, k 2 tog.

Next row; p 13.

Next row; (k 2 tog) 6 times, k 1.

Gather these last sts over the nose.

Gusset

Make this after the rest of the coverings have been fitted.

Important note: the exact size of this is important to the fit of the 'skin cover' and so the number of sts and rows must be adjusted according to the size of the gap left underneath the body. Watch for these * marks and make your adjustments where they occur.

Begin at the chest end and cast on 2sts and work 2 rows.

Now inc one st at both ends of every k row until there are * 8sts, (or less).

Purl one row. Cast on * 8 (or less) sts at beg of the next 2 rows.

Work 2 rows straight, then dec each side as folls:

Next row; k 1, sl 1, k 1, psso, k to last 3 sts, k 2 tog, k 1.

Next row; p.

Repeat these 2 rows until * 6sts rem.

Continue without shaping (if necessary) until long enough and cast off.

Making up

Pin the gusset in place (with the cast off edge at the rear) and sew to the tops of the forelegs.

Sew up the seams of the back legs and slip these on to the frame, pulling the head piece over the head and drawing up the gathering thread at the nose end. Pin all round on to the gusset and sew up with yarn and an invisible st.

Ears

Use No15/1½ mm needles, cast on 6 sts and work in ss for 6 rows.

Next row; k 2 tog, k 2, k 2 tog.

Next row; p.

Next row; (k 2 tog) twice.

Cast off, fold in half lengthwise and sew on to the head. Make 2.

Tail

This is a long tassel which has been bound round the top part for 1 in/2.5 cm to shape it. Fix it high up on to the horse's back end as shown, and trim so that the tassel is shorter on the underside.

Mane

Make a very thick plait long enough to reach from the base of the neck to well over the forehead. Tie it off between the ears, leaving ends of about 1 in/2 cm hanging free to form the forelock. Sew this in place with firm back sts.

OTHER DETAILS

The white blaze can be made by knitting a small oblong of white yarn and sewing it down the centre of the face. White socks can also be made in this way and sewn on afterwards. The eyes are large and dark: sew them well up on the head as shown.

HARNESS AND TRAPPINGS

The bridle and reins are made of short lengths of crochet chain, and a length of knitted cast-on and cast-off stitches. These short lengths are then sewn together and on to the horse's head. The blue decoration on the reins are small oblongs of gt s made on 20sts and 6 rows (size No14/2 mm needles) and these are then sewn on to the reins.

Brown horse's blue and yellow coat

Using 4 ply yarn and No10/3¼ mm needles, work from the chart on page 54. The white saddle is knitted into the coat, and has been outlined with a line of yellow chain st.

The little stirrups to keep the knight's feet in place are simply chained loops which are sewn firmly into the

The white horse is saddled and bridled and waits patiently for the prince.

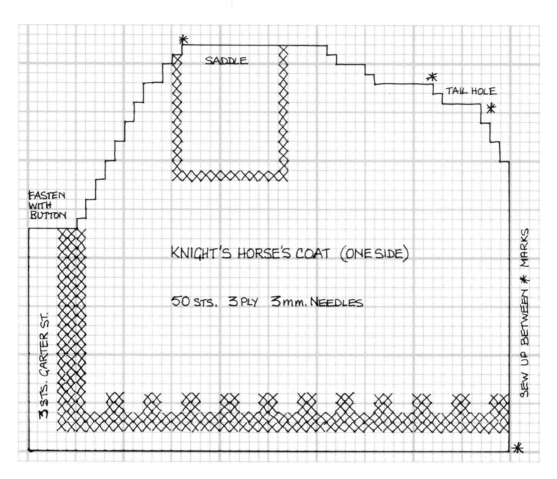

The diagram shows labels:
- SADDLE
- TAIL HOLE
- FASTEN WITH BUTTON
- KNIGHT'S HORSE'S COAT (ONE SIDE)
- 50 STS. 3 PLY 3mm. NEEDLES
- 3 STS. GARTER ST.
- SEW UP BETWEEN * MARKS

Fig 27: diagram for the horse's coat

corners of the saddle patch on the horse's coat.

The horse's coat is made in two pieces which are then sewn together along the top edges. Sew down the back edges from * to * leaving the rest open for the tail. You may need to gather this hole up with a running thread to fit on to the back. Leave the front edges open, and fasten at the neck with a gold or silver button for decoration.

White horse's saddle

Use 4 ply yarn and size No13/2¼ mm needles.

Cast on 8sts and work in gt s. Work 1 row, then inc one st at each end of 2nd row, knit the 3rd row, and on the 4th row inc again as on the 2nd, (12sts).

Work straight for 3 in/7.5 cm from the beg.

Dec one st at each end of next 2 alt rows, (8sts), then cast off 2sts at beg of next 2 rows. Continue on the rem 4sts for the girth, until this is long enough to pass under the body to the other side of the saddle. Make the stirrups as for the blue and yellow coat.

Witch and black cat

Traditionally, witches appear in black and sombre colours, but our version is more colourful and wears a very dark purple over-dress which has lighter cuffs and border, and under this she wears a multiple coloured skirt over dark leg coverings. Make her leg coverings first, at the same time as her face and hand covers. Then embroider her face (not too pretty) and knit her grey hair, as this helps to give her a certain character before you make her clothes. Keep her wrapped up warm while you're doing this, as witches get cross easily!

You will need No14/2 mm and No13/2¼ mm needles; small amounts of dark purple 3 ply (or dark grey) for the over-dress and random-dyed yarn for the under-skirt. Also small amounts of mid-purple and dark yarn for the dress and legs. Grey 3 ply for the hair and black for the hat. Oddments of yarns for the features.

The cat is made in rev ss in dark charcoal, 3 ply, and a

*The wicked witch and her cat cast spells under
the pom-pon bush in the magic forest.*

tiny amount of green will be needed for the eyes and white for the whiskers.

For the broomstick you will need oddments of brown yarn and thin wire.

HAIR AND HAT

This is knitted all in one piece.

Begin with the hair; using grey yarn and No13/2¼ mm needles, cast on 22sts and work in single rib for 12 rows.

Row 13; k 2 tog all along the row, (11sts).

Row 14; change to black yarn and p one row.

Continue in ss as follows for the top of the hat: work 6 rows straight, then (k 2 tog, k 1) to last 2sts, k 2 tog. Work 3 rows straight, then (k 2 tog) 3 times to last st, k1. P one row, then (k 2 tog) twice. Cast off.

Sew up the black point, leaving the grey hair open to frame the face. Now make the brim as follows: with black yarn, cast on 30sts and k 3 rows.

Next row; (k 1, k 2 tog) 10 times, then k one more row. Next row; (k 2 tog, k 3) 4 times. Cast off loosely.

Sew up the 2 short sides to form a circle. Stitch the hair on to the witch's head, pulling it well down, then slip the brim over and sew, making sure that no grey hair shows on top.

SKIRT

In random-dyed 3 ply yarn and with size No13/2¼mm needles, cast on 30sts and work 3 rows in gt s. Change to ss and work 25 more rows, or until long enough to reach from waist to mid-calf, (i.e. not quite full-length).

Next row; (k 1, k 2 tog) 10 times.

Cast off p-wise. Sew up the back seam, gather the top edge and sew round the waist.

OVER-DRESS

Using the same needles and mid-purple yarn, cast on 36sts and work 4 rows in gt s (beginning at the lower edge), then continue in ss for 6 more rows. (If you wish, introduce a few rows of rev ss among these 6.) In the next k row, change to dark-purple yarn, and work 2 more rows.

Next row; k 2 tog to the end of the row, (18sts), then work 11 more rows in ss.

Divide the sts into sets of 5, 8, and 5sts for the armholes. Work on these sets of sts separately for 9 rows each. Work a k row across all sts and then cast off.

Fit this on to the body and sew up the back seam.

Sleeves

Use mid-purple for the cuffs and cast on 10sts. Work 2 rows in gt s then change to dark-purple and work 9 rows in ss. Cast off. Make 2. Sew up the side seams, slip the sleeves on to the arms and sew the dress around the armholes.

BROOM

2 pcs twisted tightly together will make the broom handle. Bend the doubled ends over top and bottom and wrap tightly with brown yarn. Tie together a bundle of trimmed thin wire and attach to one end of the handle with a length of brown yarn.

CAT

The diagram above shows the pc frame used for the cat. You will need about 4 pcs and the frame should be slightly padded and wrapped to give the shape.

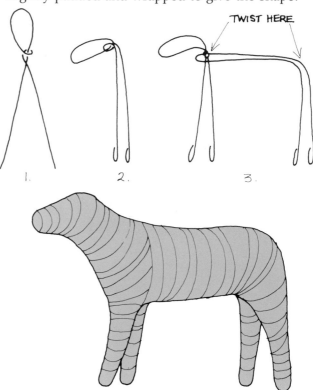

Fig 28: making the wire frame and padding the body of the cat

Using dark charcoal yarn and No14/2 mm needles cast on 10sts and work in rev ss for 6 rows. Cast on 4sts at the beg of next row and work straight for 8 rows. Cast off 4sts at the beg of next row and work straight for 6 rows. Cast off.

Slip the knitted cover over the padded body; sew over the head first, and run a thread around the neck to gather in. Stitch down the chest and gather a thread round the back edge to fit over the hindquarters as far as the legs.

Now make 4 legs: on 5sts, work in rev ss for about 10 rows (measure for exact size). Now sew these up and attach to the top of the cat's body.

The ears can be embroidered more easily than knitted. Use double yarn and make two or three sts leaving a tiny loop with each one, then take several sts into these loops, over and over, until large enough. Make the tail from a crochet chain using a fine hook and 3 strands of yarn. Embroider the eyes in green and sew on some long white whiskers.

Wizard

True to tradition, the wizard must *look* magical, and so he wears a long gown of bright colours and a tall pointed cap, though magicians do vary and you may have other ideas. His skin shows only on face and hands, as his legs and feet are covered in brown. The overgown takes the form of a long waistcoat, as the sleeves of this outer garment and those of the under-gown are knitted in one piece. The overgown is split up the sides as far as the armholes.

You will need No14/2 mm and No13/2¼ mm needles;

The wizard rests under the shade of a blossom tree as he journeys through the magic forest.

small amounts of 3 ply turquoise for the undergown, and 3 ply random-dyed yarn for the overgown. If you cannot obtain this, try using a plain 3 ply together with a fine glittery yarn, but check the measurements as you go along. Red 3 ply was used for the hat (a very small amount), brown 3 ply for the legs and feet, metallic yarn for the buckle, white 2 ply for the hair and beard, and oddments for the features. 3 ply white yarn with a glitter thread running through it was used for the staff.

You will also need a large pretty sequin, or bead, for the jewel in the hat and some glue. You may like him to wear a heavy chain and jewel around his neck, or dress him in black and cover him in sparkling sequins.

OVERGOWN

Use No13/2¼ mm needles and random-dyed yarn; begin at the back and cast on 18sts. Work 32 rows in ss, then cast off 3sts at beg of next 2 rows. Dec one st at each end of foll 2 k rows, (8sts). Work 5 more rows and leave these 8sts on a pin.

For the left front, cast on 9sts and work in ss for 32 rows but k the last 2 sts of every row. Cast off 3 sts at beg of 33rd row. Dec one st at beg of next 2 k rows. Work 6 more rows then leave these 4sts on a pin.

For the right front, use the same instructions as for the left front *except* that the first 2sts of every row should be knitted. Reverse the armhole shaping. Place all three pieces back on to the needle (in the right order, armhole to armhole) and k across all sts. (in gt s) for 4 rows, dec at both ends of the last row, then cast off.

Sleeves

Darn all ends in, then with RS facing and random-yarn, pick up 22sts around the armhole and work 4 rows in ss and 2 rows in rev ss. Chage to the same colour yarn as the undergown and p 2 tog all along the row, (11sts). Work in ss to the wrist, about 3 rows, then cast off. Make 2.

Darn ends in and press gently, sew up the lower sleeve edge and then the overgown sleeves, leaving about 2 in/5 cm open up the sides of the gown.

UNDERGOWN

Cast on 16sts and work 24 rows in ss. You may wish to insert a few rows of moss st here and there to add to the texture.

On the 25th row, k 2 tog at both ends, and repeat this on the 27th, 29th and 31st row, (8sts).
P alternate rows.
Continue in ss until the head is reached (about 10–12 rows) and cast off.
Make another piece in the same way. Press and sew up the side seams from the hem to ¾ in/2 cm from the top. Slip the undergown on to the figure and sew up the shoulders. Now fit the overgown on top of this and decorate with a large buckle as folls: use gold metallic yarn and cast on 10sts. Knit 3 rows in gt s and cast off, then gather one long edge into a circle. Glue this in place.

BEARD

In the white yarn, and size No14/2 mm needles, cast on 5sts and work in single rib for 6 rows. Inc one st at each end of the next 4 rows, (13sts).
Work 2 more rows in rib, then cast off in rib. Sew this round the lower face from ear to ear.

HAIR AND FACE

Cast on 20sts and work in single rib for 8 rows. Cast off in rib and sew one long edge around the head, leaving a bald patch on top. Embroider a pink nose, 2 blue eyes and thick white eyebrows.

HAT

Use No13/2¼ mm needles and cast on 28sts. Work 4 rows in ss.
5th row; (k 2 tog, k 5) 4 times.
6th and alt rows;p.
7th row; (k 2 tog, k 4) 4 times.
9th row; (k 2 tog, k 3) 4 times.
11th row; (k 2 tog, k 2) 4 times.
13th row; (k 2 tog, k 1) 4 times, (8sts).
Work 5 more rows in ss then (k 2 tog) 4 times.
Draw the last sts on to a thread and sew up. Allow the brim to curl upwards at the front, and sew on to the head with a firm back st.

STAFF

1 pc, doubled over at either end, will make the staff. Wrap tightly with the glittery yarn and sew it on to the wizard's hand.

MAGIC FOREST

*Fairy folk, trolls, witches and
mythical creatures live in toadstool homes
and beneath talking trees,
deep in the heart of the magic forest.*

FOREST

The magic forest is a perfect setting for the enchanted folk. Use lovely glittery yarns to create a magical effect.

Talking trees

The talking trees are enchanted creatures who were changed into trees by a magic spell and are waiting to be freed from their tree-bodies. They stand about 12 in/30 cm tall and the general pattern can be adpated in any way you choose, by colour, yarn texture, size and shape.

You will need No8/4 mm needles; any yarns, but double-knitting (DK) or thicker, is best - greens, browns and greys; cardboard tubes, about 9 in/23 cm tall with a diameter of 1¼ in/3 cm, a circular piece of thick card for the stand, about 3 in/8 cm diameter, either dark brown or dark green.

You will also need pliable but strong wire; for each tree you will need 4 pieces, each one about 20 in/51 cm long and one piece about 30 in/76 cm long, and a small pair of pliers and glue. Strong linen tape would be useful, but not essential, and a small amount of padding for the feet.

TO MAKE THE FRAME

1. Stick the base of the tube to the circle of card and allow to set (see Fig 29).]
2. Make the wire branches as folls:
   (a) Bend each piece of wire in half and bend the cut ends down with pliers, about ¾ in/2 cm and twist the 2 halves together to strengthen.
   (b) Make 8 small holes about ½ in/1.5 cm down from the top edge of the tube, just big enough to allow the doubled wires to pass through and no more. Space these equally apart.
   (c) Push the 4 wire pieces through the holes from one side to the other, so that there are 8 branches sticking out all round. Using the pliers, these should now be bent upwards to a vertical position for the time being. Do not tear the card while you are doing this!
   (d) At this point, wrap the linen tape once or twice round the top, over the wires and holes to strengthen this part.

KNITTED TREE COVER

This is the pattern for the moss stitch tree; the cable tree will need more sts and a cable needle.

Cast on loosely. Make a piece of knitted fabric to cover the tube, the above size will need a piece 4 in/10 cm wide. If thick DK yarn is used, and size 4 mm needles, 20sts will be needed. Finer yarn and/or needles will require more sts. Work in any textured st, such as double moss st or cables, and make the nose as follows:

Next row; patt 9sts, then inc 5sts into one st by making a k 1, p 1, k 1, p 1, k 1 all into the same st.

Knit 4 or 5 rows on these 5sts only, then dec back to one again. Continue along the row to the end.

Continue working to the top of the tube and then divide for the branches. Divide for 8 branches (for

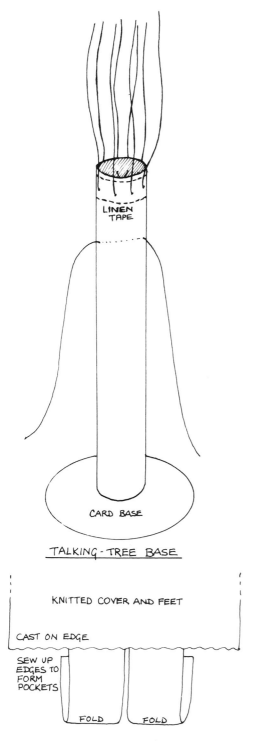

Fig 29: making the base for the talking trees

more than 20sts, adjust accordingly). Keep the 20sts on a stitch-holder or pin, and work 8 sets of sts individually, 4 sets of 3, and 4 sets of 2 *but* increase one st at the start of each set of 2 to make 3sts. These knitted branches should be as long as the wire branches and will enclose them when the tube is attached to the trunk. Use any st for the branches, garter or stocking. When casting off the 3sts, leave a long enough end of yarn to sew along each branch. When all 8 branches have been knitted, make the feet as follows.

Feet

Turn to the bottom of the knitted tree-cover and with the RS facing count 4sts in from the edge and pick up the next 5sts (i.e. from the cast-on edge) and knit 26 rows in gt s. Cast off, and pick up the next 5sts in the centre and knit another strip of 26 rows. Fold the strips in half and sew the two sides up, place a little padding inside the pocket thus formed and sew the cast-off edge to the trunk base (see Fig 29).

Making up

Take the piece of long wire and fold it in half, bending the 2 cut ends and twisting together as before. Make holes in each side of the card tube, about 2 in/5 cm from the top and insert the wire through the knitted cover and the card tube at the same time before sewing up. Pin the cover on to the tube and sew up the back seam, then enclose each wire branch in its knitted cover, fastening off each one securely. Bind each wire arm (i.e. the 2 lower ones) tightly round with thick oddments of yarn until the upper arm is as thick as a pencil and the lower part slightly thinner.

Now knit 2 covers for these arms with the same yarn as before, casting on about 34sts and working about 6 rows in ss, using the rev side as the RS. To make the piece wider at one end, k half a row, turn and p back. This will give 2 extra rows at one end. Position the coverings over the arms and pin in place, then sew firmly, stitching into the trunk at the 'shoulder' end. Embroider the eyes and mouth as shown.

Glue the lower edge of the trunk covering and the feet to the card base. Make a large floppy pom-pon using coarse green yarn and glue this to the top of the trunk inside the branches, pulling the ends well down over the head.

Small trees and bushes

These are perhaps the simplest of all to make. Cover a toilet-roll tube with a simple oblong of knitting, using gt s, ss, rev ss, or a textured yarn. Sew the two edges together and glue the piece in place, then add a huge, thick pom-pon of green, green/brown, russet or blossom-pink yarn. If the tree falls over easily, cut a small circle of thick card and glue this on to the base. The card tubes can be cut in half to make bushes. The pom-pons are glued to the tops.

Toadstool house

This can be seen on page 79. The overall height of the toadstool house is 7½ in/19 cm and its diameter is just over 6 in/15 cm. A circle of card will be needed for stiffening the top part, measuring 6 in/15 cm diameter exactly, and double-knitting yarns are used for the coverings, door and window, etc. Padding will be needed for the domed top.

TOP OF TOADSTOOL

Using gold-coloured yarn and size No10/3¼ mm needles, cast on 106sts, and work 10 rows in ss.
Row 11; (k 2 tog, k 8) 10 times, k 2 tog, k 4.
Row 12; purl on alternate rows.
Row 13; (k 2 tog, k 3) 19 times, (76 sts).
Row 15; (k 2 tog, k 3) 15 times, k 1, (61 sts).
Row 17; (k 2 tog, k 3) 12 times, k 1, (49 sts).
Row 19; (k 2 tog, k 3) 9 times, k 2 tog, k 2, (39 sts).
Row 21; (k 2 tog, k 6) 4 times, k 2 tog, k 5, (34 sts).
Row 23; (k 2 tog, k 6) 4 times, k 2 tog, (29 sts).

Row 25; (k 2 tog, k 6) 3 times, k 3, (25 sts).
Row 27; (k 2 tog, k 6) 3 times, k 1, (22 sts).
Row 29; (k 2 tog, k 2) 5 times, k 2 tog, (16 sts).
Row 31; (k 2 tog) 8 times, (8 sts). Draw these sts up to form the top, and stitch the two side edges together.

GILLS

Using brown yarn and size No10/3¼ mm needles, cast on 100 sts and work 10 rows, or 1¼ in/3.5 cm. Cast off and sew up the side seams.

STALK

Using stone coloured yarn, cast on 55sts and work in ss for about 5 in/13 cm. Cast off and sew up the side seams, slip this on to a tube of card. Assemble as shown in the diagram.

well over to the underside, holding it in place with pins. Lace across the back.

GILLS

In dark brown yarn, cast on 52sts using the same needles.
Work in k 2, p 2 rib for 8 rows, cast off in rib and sew up the two side seams.
Sew the cast on edge to the outer edge of the top.

STALKS

This is for a card tube which measures 2½ in long × 1½ in diameter/6.5 cm × 4 cm. Make a rectangle of fabric approximately 5½ in × 2½ in/14 cm × 6.5 cm. This one needs 34sts, double-knitting yarn, size No10/3¼ mm needles and 20 rows, but this should be checked against the tube.
See the diagram for assembling instructions.

Small toadstools

These can be seen on page 68 and 71.

TOP OF TOADSTOOLS

Using double-knitting yarn, and size No10/3¼ mm needles, cast on 50 sts and work 8 rows in ss. Then proceed as follows;
Row 9; (k 2 tog, k 3) 10 times, (40 sts).
Work 5 more rows in ss.
Row 15; (k 2 tog, k 2) 10 times, (30 sts).
Work 3 more rows in ss.
Row 19; (k 2 tog, k 1) 10 times, and purl the next row.
Row 21; (k 2 tog) 10 times.
Finish off by drawing a thread through the last sts and sewing up the two sides. Now cut a circle of stiff card 4 in/10 cm diameter, and stick a thick layer of padding to one side. Place the knitted top over this, and pull

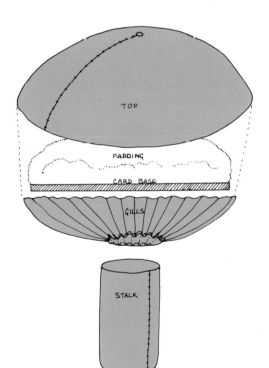

Fig 30: assembling the toadstool

FIGURES

Let your imagination run riot with a beautiful mixture of sparkling yarns. Instructions for making the wire frame bodies and knitted body coverings of the fairy folk are shown on pages 42 and 43. Picot pattern is used on some of the figures, see page 68. The diagrams for the wings shown on page 66 are general instructions and apply to all the fairies and elves.

*Oberon and Titania have discovered the Irish leprechaun
taking a rest under a bluebell.*

Fairy Wings

Take an 11 in/28 cm length of firm but bendable wire and twist the ends together as shown in *a*.
Shape into 2 wing-shapes – *b* – and twist each side once or twice – *c*.
Knit a rectangle of fine, glittery yarn just big enough to cover the wing area – *d*.
Attach the two outside edges of the knitting to the wire frame – *e*.
Gather the central area down towards the twisted parts – *f* – and continue to oversew the edges all the way round until the wire is completely covered.
Light, sparkling effects are obtained by combining fine crochet threads and fine gold threads made for machine sewing. Use size No10/3¼ mm needles to create a lacy, open effect.
The position of the wings on the fairy's shoulders are shown in *g*. Sew these very firmly.

Titania

Titania can be seen on page 65.

BODICE

A rectangle made in a mixture of a very fine Shetland wool, and any fine sparkling yarn.
Use size No15/1½ mm needles. Cast on 11sts, work 16 rows ss. Make 2 pieces and join at the shoulders and down the sides.

Stand-up collar

Size No15/1½ mm needles, any fine glitter yarn. Cast on 12sts. K 2 rows.
3rd row; inc into every other st all along the row.
K 2 more rows then change needles to size No10/3¼ mm, k 2 more rows and cast off. Sew the narrow edge around the neck, attaching the side edges to the shoulders.

SKIRT

Same yarn as bodice, No12/2¾ mm needles. Cast on 40sts.
Work 2 rows in ss then change to size No7/4½ mm

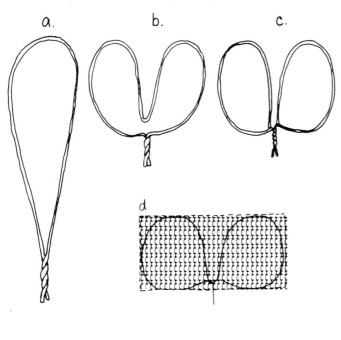

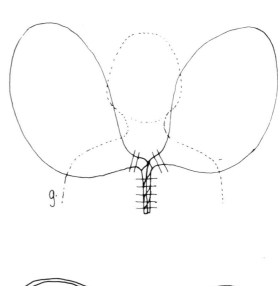

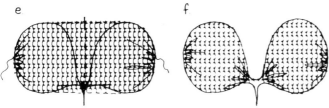

Fig 31: diagrams for wings

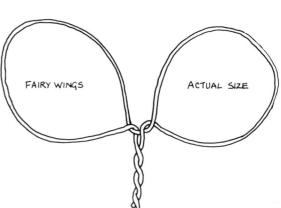

FAIRY WINGS   ACTUAL SIZE

needles. Continue to the bottom for an ankle length skirt, introducing a band of gold yarn towards the last few rows.

UNDERSKIRT

This is a straight tube of fine white yarn from waist to ankles. Gather it around the waist and sew in place, then gather the top skirt and sew this over the top.

HAIR

This is a little cap of fine white moss st, (every row k 1, p 1 on an odd number of sts) shaped like a long rectangle. Size No14/2 mm needles. Cast on 25sts, and work 8–10 rows. Do not cast off but gather the last sts up to form the top of the hair, sew up the side edges and fit the cap well down on to the head. This is topped by a similar cap of glitter yarn, over which a crocheted chain band of gold thread has been sewn to resemble a delicate crown.

WINGS

Titania wears two pairs of wings, one of them smaller than the usual size, and these are covered loosely in a combination of crochet thread and fine glitter sewing thread.

WAND

Wrap a piece of fine wire with white yarn, folding the ends over sharply so that they are covered with yarn. Attach loops of glitter yarn to one end, then cut these to give a sparkling effect. Sequins may be added here and there.

Oberon

Oberon can be seen on page 64. The leg covering is of fine white yarn combined with metallic thread.

TUNIC

Made of double metallic thread. On size No15/1½ mm needles cast on 20sts.
Work in ss straight from hips to armholes, then divide for the arms.
Work 11 rows on the first 5sts.
Work 11 rows on the centre 10sts (this is the front).
Work 10 rows on the next 5sts, then k across all sts, thread these on to a length of yarn and gather. Slip the tunic on to the figure and sew up the back with the neck thread.

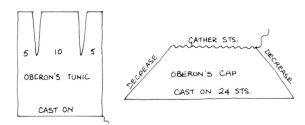

Fig 32: Oberon's tunic and cap

Collar

This is a crocheted braid of gold yarn fixed with a large sequin.

CAP

Cast on loosely, 24sts with silver yarn, and knit in ss to the shape shown in the diagram. Gather the last sts.

WINGS

Two pairs, one large and one small, made of glitter yarn and decorated with large silver sequins. Oberon's wings are about twice as big as the fairy's wings.

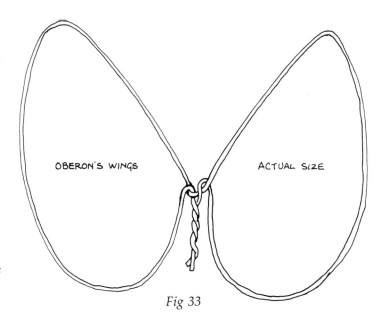

Fig 33

*The snowflake fairy's dress sparkles like the snow
and her tiny bonnet keeps her ears warm in the biting frost.*

Snowflake fairy

The leg covering is of fine white yarn. Picot pattern is used in her dress. It is worked as follows.

PICOT PATTERN

1st row; wool round needle to make one st, then *k 2 tog, and yarn forward* all along the row to the end, finishing with k 2 tog.

2nd row; purl.

These two rows form the pattern, making a row of holes which can be left open to make a lacy stitch, or folded over to make a pointed hem.

DRESS

White 2 ply baby wool combined with fine glitter yarn, with No15/1½ mm needles cast on 16sts. Work 4 rows in ss, then change to 2 rows of picot patt then work 14 more rows of ss.

Next row; k 2 tog all along the row, (8sts).

Next row; k 1, p 1.

Next row; change to aquamarine yarn and p 1, k 1. Continue in moss st for 6 rows then cast off. Make another piece in the same way. The front and back of the dress must now be completed *on the figure* as the

neck is not designed to fit over the head. Attach the back and front at one shoulder with 2sts, then fit these on to the figure and attach the shoulders at the other side. Leave the side seams free for the moment, these will be sewn up at the same time as the sleeve seam.

Sleeves

Using fine glitter yarn and aquamarine yarn, cast on 10sts and work in ss for 4 rows. Change to white yarn with glitter yarn.

Increase into every st (20sts) and work 5 more rows in ss.

Now work 2 rows of picot patt and cast off.

Sew up the sleeve seams, slip on to the arms and sew invisibly into the bodice, completing the side seam as you go.

HEAD-DRESS

Use fine white 2 ply and fine glitter yarn on No15/1½ mm needles.

Cast on 20sts and work 4 rows in ss then 2 rows picot patt and 8 more rows of ss. Gather the last sts on to a length of yarn and draw up. This is the back of the head-dress. Catch the two edges together with 2 or 3sts, and sew up half of the side edges – this gap fits around the back of the neck, with the cast-on edge framing the face. Sew in place and decorate the points of the picots with tiny pearl beads.

WINGS

She wears two small pairs of wings, one knitted with fine silver yarn and the other in white yarn but bound round the edges with fine silver yarn. Large needles give the openwork effect.

Daisy elf

Daisy and Daffodil elf are just two of the possibilities illustrated on the basic 'flower fairy' theme, wearing a simple tunic and hat, with leg coverings of the appropriate colour.

TUNIC

Random-dyed green 3 ply yarn, size No15/1½ mm needles. Make two pieces the same.

Cast on 14sts, work 16 rows of ss.

17th row; k 2 tog across all sts (7sts) then work 8 rows on these sts. Cast off. Sew up the sides from bottom to top as far as the decrease row, leaving the top part open for the arms. Stitch across the shoulders at x – 2 or 3 long sts should stretch across a gap of about ¼ in/1 cm which will be covered by the collar.

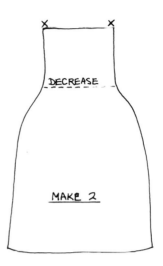

Fig 34: tunic for daisy elf

Collar

Green embroidery wool with fine glitter yarn.

Size No15/1½ mm needles, 20sts and 4 rows of ss.

Then work 2 rows of picot patt, and 6 more rows of ss. Fold up the picot hem and stitch in place, sew up the side edges and gather the cast on edge to fit around the neck. Sew in position.

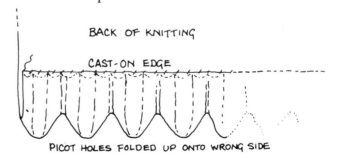

Fig 35: picot hem

DAISY HAT

Beginning with the yellow centre use 3 ply yarn and size No13/2¼ mm needles. Cast on 14sts and work 4 rows of ss.

Next row; k 2 tog all along the row (7sts) and gather these on to a length of yarn, sew up the side edges and stitch the cap to the top of the head.

Petal brim: use fine 2 ply white yarn combined with fine glitter yarn on size No13/2¼ mm needles. Cast on 28sts and work 6 rows in ss.

Work 2 rows in picot patt and then 8 more rows in ss. Fold up the picot hem and stitch in place and sew up the side seams. Gather the edge and sew this to the yellow crown of the hat, all the way round.

WINGS

Gold yarn.

Size No10/3¼ mm needles. Cast on 10sts and work 22 rows, (see page 66).

Daffodil elf

TUNIC

Yellow 3 ply yarn, size No10/3¼ mm needles.
Cast on 28sts, work 4 rows of ss, then 2 rows of picot patt.
Work 5 rows of single rib, beginning with a p st, then change needles to size No13/2¼ mm and rib 5 more rows.
Divide for the armholes: work 7 rows each on three divisions of 7, 14, and 7sts.

Gather the last sts on to a length of yarn and gather around the neck. Sew up the back seam.

HAT

Embroidery wool in orange, used double.
Size No13/2¼ mm needles. Cast on 20sts, work 4 rows of ss.
Next row; (k 2 tog, k 2) 5 times (15 sts).
P alternate rows.

The daffodil elf and the daisy elf take turns to ride on the ladybird,
who enjoys the fun as much as they do.

Forest elf lives among the trees and fungi of the woodlands.

Next row; (k 2 tog, k 1) 5 times.
Next row; (k 2 tog) to end of the row (5sts).
Draw these sts on to a length of yarn and sew up the side seam.

WINGS
These are the same as for the Daisy elf.

Forest elf

Mid-green leg covering.

TUNIC
Fine, pale green 3 ply yarn, size No13/2¼ mm needles.
Cast on 16sts, work 4 rows of ss, then change to picot patt for 12 rows, or as far as the armholes. Cast off.

Sleeves and top

These are made in one piece from one sleeve edge to the other. Cast on 14sts and work 4 rows in ss. Change to picot patt for 2 rows, * then work 6 more rows of ss. Divide for the neck opening: k 6, cast off 2sts, k 6. Work ss for 9 rows on each set of 6sts, then join across as follows: k 6, turn, and cast on 2sts, turn again, k 6. Purl across all 14sts. Now work in ss for 6 more rows, then 2 rows of picot patt, then 4 more rows of ss. Cast off and press lightly.

Fold up the picot hem on the sleeves, and sew up each sleeve seam *only* on the folded part of the hems, leaving the rest open for the lower tunic. Slip this part of the costume on to the figure. Sew up the back seam of the lower tunic, and slip this on to the figure, feet first. Sew the 2 pieces together from the right side. Stitch the neckline on to the figure, gathering it in a little at the same time if necessary.

HAT

Fine green 3 ply yarn, size No13/2¼mm needles.
Cast on 18sts, work in ss for 4 rows.
Next row; (k 4, k 2 tog) 3 times.
Purl alternate rows.
Next row; (k 3, k 2 tog) 3 times.
Next row; (k 2 tog) to the end of the row, then gather these sts on to a length of yarn and sew the 2 side edges together. Sew the hat well down on to the head.

WINGS

One strand green embroidery wool combined with fine glitter yarn.
Size No10/3¼mm needles.

Water elf

Two different tones of blue have been used for the leg covering in embroidery wool

TUNIC

The basic instructions for the tunic are the same as for the Forest elf, but here, the reverse of the fabric (the purl side) is the right side. However, the picot edge on the sleeves is still on the smooth side, so the following notes should be read before commencing.

Three strands of yarn were used together, 2 of embroidery wool (one blue and one white) and one strand of fine glitter yarn. Two different blues were interchanged at times to try to indicate a subtle movement of colour. Small pearls can either be threaded on to the yarn and knitted in, or sewn on afterwards.

Sleeves

White 2 ply baby yarn combined with fine glitter yarn. Work as for the Forest elf as far as *, then work 2 rows in ss.

Change to reverse ss by purling the next row and knitting the one after that until 8–9 rows after the picot patt are complete (i.e. instead of 6). Continue as for Forest elf but now read 'knit' instead of 'purl' and vice versa. Work rev ss for 6 rows on second sleeve, then change to ss by knitting row 7 and purling row 8.

Work 2 rows of picot patt, then 4 rows of ss. Cast off and press lightly.

Turn picot hems up on sleeve edges, remembering that you are using the reverse side of the fabric as the right side in this version. Finish off as for the Forest elf.

HAT

White 2 ply baby yarn combined with fine glitter yarn. This version is more pointed than the Forest elf's.
Cast on 18sts using No13/2¼mm needles. Work ss for 8 rows, then continue as follows, purling on alternate rows;
Row 9; (k 4, k 2 tog) 3 times.
Row 11; (k 3, k 2 tog) 3 times.
Row 13; (k 2, k 2 tog) 3 times.
Row 15; (k 1, k 2 tog) 3 times (6sts).
Row 17; (k 2 tog) 3 times. Gather the last 3sts on to a thread and sew up.
Complete as for the Forest elf.

WINGS

As for the Forest elf, using blue yarn.

*Water elf likes to wander near flowing streams
and rivers, waterfalls and meadow ponds.*

The gnome and his wife are industrious little creatures
who enjoy the warmth of a log fire when work is done.

Gnome husband

Mid-green leg covering. Some padding inside the tunic will be needed to give the gnome a more rotund frame than the delicate fairies.

TUNIC

This is better explained in the diagram opposite as it is made in one complete piece, folded across the shoulders. A 3 ply yarn was used for this on size No14/2 mm needles.

Belt

This is made on 3 sts in 3 ply yarn on size No15/1½ mm needles, in gt s. Make it long enough to go round the hips and sew the ends together at the back. The buckle is from a bra strap!

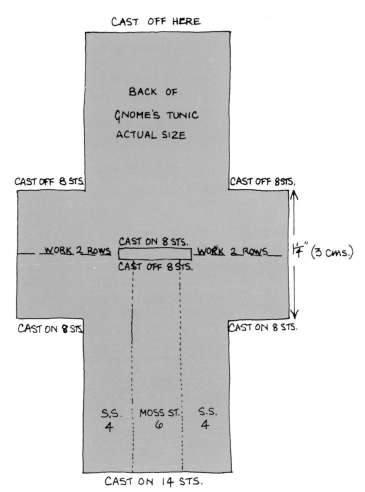

CAST OFF HERE

BACK OF
GNOME'S TUNIC
ACTUAL SIZE

CAST OFF 8 STS.   CAST OFF 8 STS.

WORK 2 ROWS   CAST ON 8 STS.   WORK 2 ROWS   1¼" (3 CMS.)
               CAST OFF 8 STS.

CAST ON 8 STS.   CAST ON 8 STS.

S.S.   MOSS ST.   S.S.
4   6   4

CAST ON 14 STS.

Fig 36: knitted tunic for the gnome

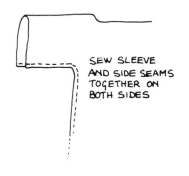

SEW SLEEVE
AND SIDE SEAMS
TOGETHER ON
BOTH SIDES

HAT

Cast on 20sts in 3 ply yarn on No15/1½ mm needles, work in ss for 8 rows, then:
Row 9; k 2 tog, k 7, k 2 tog, k 7, k 2 tog.
Purl on alternate rows.
Row 11; k 2 tog, k 5, k 2 tog, k 5, k 2 tog, k 1.
Row 13; k 2 tog, k 4, k 2 tog, k 4, k 2 tog.
Row 15; k 2 tog, k 2, k 2 tog, k 2, k 2 tog, k 1. *
Row 17; (k 2 tog) 4 times (4sts).
Gather the sts on to a length of yarn, draw up and sew the sides together.

BAG

Use 3 ply brown yarn on No15/1½ mm needles. Work in ss for 20 rows on 7sts. Now decrease one st at each end of the next 2 knit rows, then p one more row. Cast off the last 3sts, sew up the sides and stitch the flap down. Make a strap of crochet chain.

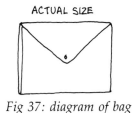

ACTUAL SIZE

Fig 37: diagram of bag

BOOTS

Use brown 2 ply baby wool, cast on 14sts on No15/1½ mm needles, work in ss for 20 rows. Thread the last sts on to the yarn and gather up to form the toe. Make another one to match.

Gnome wife

BODICE

The length of this should be measured against the figure for exact results. It consists of 2 small rectangles, one each for the front and back, joined at the shoulders leaving a space for the head to go through. Use 3 ply yarn and No15/1½ mm needles. Cast on 10sts.
The short sleeves are 2 shallow rectangles of 10sts and 6 rows. These are joined to the bodice across the shoulders before the side and sleeve seams are sewn up. The white cuffs are of 2 ply wool on size No15/1½ mm needles. Cast on 20sts. Work in ss for 10 rows, then cast off and join the side edges. Sew these to the lower edge of each sleeve.

SKIRT

This is a rectangle of grey 3 ply wool in ss. Use size No10/3¼ mm needles and cast on 30sts. Measure it against the figure from the waist to the ankles, and introduce bands of rev ss and gt s at the lower edge. Sew up the sides and gather the top edge on to the bodice.

HAT

This is the same as for her husband, but uses grey wool. She also wears a scarf under her hat, but this need only be indicated by a long narrow strip of blue or any bright colour sewn around the head under the hat.

APRON

Use any colour 3 ply wool, cast on 10sts on size No13/2¼ mm needles. Work in ss for 14 rows, then cast off and sew the top edge to the centre portion of an 8 in/20 cm crochet chain.

LACE SHAWL

Use a fine white 2 ply on size No15/1½ mm needles, cast on 22sts and work in ss for 2 rows. On the 3rd row, inc in the first, then in every 3rd st to the end of the row (30sts). Inc one st at each end of the next k row, then p the next row. Change needles to size No10/3¼ mm and work 2 rows of ss.
Work 2 rows of picot patt, making the 2nd row knit instead of purl.
Cast off. Sew on to the figure as shown in the picture.

Brownie husband

Traditionally, these helpful little people are very poorly dressed; some even wear rags, though if new clothes are made for them and left as a gift, the brownies will never be seen again, though the clothes will disappear too! These brownies are reasonably well dressed compared to some others and do not like to be either thanked or taken for granted. Those which have become displeased by the treatment they receive have sometimes turned into hobgoblins and caused great mischief instead. The leg coverings are dark brown.

SHIRT

Made in one piece with the sleeves picked up from the side edges. Use 2 ply white baby yarn and size No14/2 mm needles. Cast on 14sts and work 12 rows of ss. Divide for the neck opening, leaving 7sts on each side. Work 9 rows on each side separately, then purl across both sets to make a complete row of 14sts again (rather like a large buttonhole). Continue in ss for 19 more rows, and cast off on the 20th row.

Sleeves
Pick up 12sts from the side edges and work ss for 8 rows, then cast off.
Sew up the sleeve and side seams, slip the shirt over the head and neatly stitch the lower edge of the shirt to the body all the way round.

WAISTCOAT

Use brown embroidery wool, size No15/1½ mm needles and work on 6sts and 12 rows in gt s. Cast off 3sts and k 10 more rows. Leave these sts on a spare needle and make another piece the same. Now knit across both sets of 3sts and continue down the back (see diagram below) on 6sts for 10 rows. Cast on 4sts at the beginning of the next 2 rows (14sts) and work 12 more rows in gt s. Cast off and join the side seams.

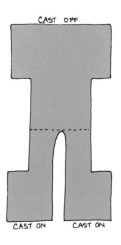

Fig 38: diagram of the brownie's waistcoat

*Once the housework is done, the brownies take
a few moments rest to admire the gleaming pans.*

HAT

This is the same as the gnome's hat except that the first
4 rows are worked in garter st.

SCARF

This version is crocheted on a foundation of 3 chains,
but it can just as easily be knitted in gt s on 3 or 4sts for
as long as you wish.

HAIR

Use 3 ply random-dyed brown wool, size No13/2¼ mm
needles. Cast on 18sts and work 4 rows of gt s.
Next row; k 2 tog all along the row (9sts) then k one
more row and gather the sts on to a length of yarn and
sew up.

Brownie wife

The brownie wife does not wear shoes. She carries a duster in her hand, a sign of her willingness to do any task around the house. (See page 77).

SKIRT

Random-dyed yarn gives this rather shabby look to the skirt, but any fine 2 ply yarn will do just as well. Cast on 40sts, using No14/2 mm needles, and work in gt s for 2 in/5 cm. Gather the top edge after sewing up the side seam.

BODICE

This is knitted sideways, and has white sleeves attached to the sides.
Using brown yarn as for the skirt, cast on 18sts with No14/2 mm needles, and work in gt s for 4 rows.
Next row; k 7, cast off 4sts, k 7 (including the one left on the needle).
Knit 5 rows on the first set of 7sts, then join the yarn to the 2nd set and work 5 rows.
Next row; k 7, cast on 4sts, k 7, across all the sts, then k 5 more rows and cast off.

Sleeves

Knitted in white 2 ply baby wool on size No14/2 mm needles. Cast on 14sts, work 14 rows in ss.
Attach the cast-on edge of the sleeves to the bodice as shown in the diagram and sew up the sleeve and bodice seams. Slip over the head on to the body and gather under the gathered edge of the skirt. Sew the two pieces together.
Slip stitch the bodice neckline on to the figure.

APRON

With 2 ply white baby wool and size No14/2 mm needles, cast on 12sts and work 12 rows of ss, then 2 rows of picot patt, then 2 rows of gt s.
Cast off and make a crochet chain of 6 in/15 cm, which is then attached to the top edge of the apron.

DUSTER

This measures 2 in/5 cm square and is knitted in yellow embroidery wool on 20sts, size No15/1½ mm needles. Work 26 rows of ss or until square. Using a crochet hook, work 2 rows of double crochet around the edge. Then press flat.

HAIR

Use red-brown embroidery wool and size No15/1½ mm needles, cast on 20sts and work in single rib for ¾ in/2 cm then ss for 6 rows. Slip the last sts on to a thread and leave for the moment. Run a gathering thread along the line between the rib and the ss, draw up and fit this to the top of the head. Sew this piece in place. Insert a tiny piece of padding into the stocking st area. Draw up the thread and sew it up to form a bun.

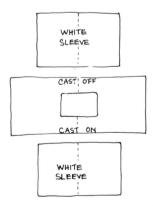

Fig 39: diagram of bodice and sleeves

Leprechaun

The lower legs are covered by white stockings and shoes knitted in one piece. Over the top edge of these he wears knee breeches. His quaint, old-fashioned dress is that of the well-known Irish fairy shoemaker, who is often seen wearing a three-cornered hat, though our version wears a simpler hat decorated with a sprig of shamrock, (see below, right).

SHIRT

Same as that of the brownie except that the sleeves have been made longer by 4 rows. Check on the basic figure to be exact about this.

KNEE BREECHES

Use a tweedy 3 ply Shetland wool in light brown, on size No13/2¼ mm needles. Cast on 12sts and work 22

The thin goblin waits for his friend to emerge from his toadstool house,
while the leprechaun joins him for a chat.

rows in ss. Make 2 pieces the same. Sew up as shown in the diagram.

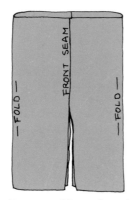

Fig 40: diagram of leprechaun's breeches

STOCKINGS AND SHOES

Using white 2 ply baby yarn and No15/1½ mm needles, cast on 14sts and work in ss for 16 rows, then change to dark brown yarn for the same thickness (double embroidery wool was used here) and work 10 more rows for the shoes. Gather the last sts on to the end of the foot and sew up. These should reach just above the knees. Sew them on to the legs, and draw the breeches over the top edge and catch them down. Run a gathering thread around the top of the shoes to draw them in to the ankles.

WAISTCOAT

This follows the same instructions as for the brownie, using green 3 ply yarn on No14/2 mm needles.

HAT

Use a 3 ply Shetland wool on size No14/2 mm needles, and cast on 18sts.
K 2 rows, p 1 row, k the next row.
Next row; (p 2 tog) 9 times (9sts), then k one more row. Cast off, then sew up and make a brim of crochet by working one double crochet into each cast off st all the way round the crown of the hat. With green wool, embroider (chain st) a band all the way round, and chain a sprig of green shamrock for his hat-band.

Thin goblin

Goblins are probably the least desirable of all the little people in this book, and traditionally they are portrayed as very ugly creatures. Our thin and fat goblins are not so much ugly as mischievous and rather cross-looking.
The leg coverings are purple.

TUNIC

This is made in a purple Shetland 3 ply on size No14/2 mm needles and 16sts. It is made to be sewn up the back. Follow the instructions as shown on the diagram, working in ss as far as the armholes (about 14 rows), then divide and work on the three sections separately for about 9 rows to the neck. Cast off and gather round the neckline.

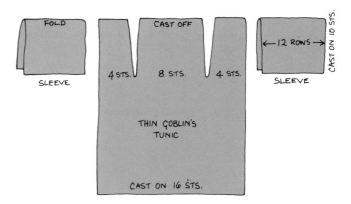

Fig 41: diagram of thin goblin's tunic

Sleeves

Cast on 10sts and work 12 rows; join the sides and stitch into the armhole of the tunic body. For the thin goblin, the tunic must be fitted on to the body before sewing up the back seam.

HAT

Use Shetland 3 ply wool on size No13/2¼ mm needles and cast on 20sts.
Work 8 rows in gt s, then follow the same instructions as for the gnome's hat as far as *, then ss for 6 rows. Then k 2 tog 4 times (4sts) and finish off. The front brim is turned up away from the face, and the back turned down.

BEARD

Use white 2 ply baby wool, size No14/2 mm needles and cast on 8sts, work 8 rows in single rib. Divide into 2 sections and work on each side separately on 4sts. Do not cast off, but gather the sts on to the cheeks underneath the hat.

The fat and thin goblins prepare to take a ride.

Fat goblin

Pad the body by wrapping it round the middle with narrow strips of padding. Bind these in position with thick yarn, (see page 81). The leg coverings are purple and the hat is the same as for the thin goblin. The beard is also the same, but it is gathered along the lower edge.

TUNIC

Follow the same instructions as for the thin goblin but double the number of sts to 32, using No13/2¼ mm needles. Knit one row and then change to size No11/3 mm needles and continue in ss for 14 rows.
Divide for the armholes 8sts–16sts–8sts.

Sleeves

The sleeves are also the same except that 12sts are worked instead of 10. Finish off in the same way as the thin goblin's version, but gather the edge of the tunic in with a thread and draw up gently towards the legs.

Belt

The belt is embroidered in chain st, using double yarn.

Rumpelstiltskin

This is the fairy character who, every night, spun heaps of straw into gold so that the young maiden could marry the king. She then found herself in the difficult position of having to guess his name. Here he is dressed in bright colours, each side of him different, as his character shows distinct traces of both charity and malevolence! He wears tights, a longish striped, multi-coloured tunic and a close-fitting hat with a pom-pon on top. His long hair and beard are the way he is usually represented.

TROUSERS

Using orange and yellow 3 ply yarns and size No14/2 mm needles, begin each leg as for the prince's breeches and boots on page 44, but working 32 rows in the same colour instead of 25 rows, and draw the last row up to form the toe.

TUNIC

The front and back are the same.
With No14/2 mm needles and orange, yellow and purple 3 ply yarns, cast on 12sts, beg at top and work 20 rows in ss (striped in 5 bands of 4 rows each). Change colour on a k row, then work 5 rows of single rib. Cast off in rib and make another piece in the same way.
Place the 2 pieces RS tog and make 2 or 3 sewing sts on each side of the shoulder seam, allowing enough room for the head to go through the opening.
With RS facing, pick up 14sts from the base of the 3rd stripe (i.e. from the shoulder) to the base of the 3rd stripe on the other side, along the side edge of the knitting. This is for the sleeve. Begin with a p row, and work 7 (striped) rows in ss.
8th row; (k 2 tog, k 1) 4 times, k 2 tog.
9th row; p.
Cast off, and work the other side in the same way.
Fold the garment RS's together and sew sleeve and side seams. Fit the tunic on to the figure and sl st the welt to the top of the legs, or leave free.

HAT

With No14/2 mm needles and 3 ply yarn, cast on 28sts, begin with a k row and work in rev ss for 2 rows, then change colour and work in ss (begin with a p row) for 5 rows.
Next row; (k 2 tog) 14 times.
Next row; p.
Next row; (k 2 tog) 7 times.
Thread these 7sts on to a length of yarn and gather up, using the same yarn to sew up the 2 edges for the back seam. Make a pom-pon of contrasting yarn and sew this to the top.

The troll and Rumpelstiltskin plot mischief under the pom-pon bush.

HAIR

With white yarn and size No14/2 mm needles cast on 18sts and work in single rib for 7 rows. Change to size No12/2¾ mm needles and work 2 more rows, then change to size No8/4 mm needles and work 4 more rows.

Next row; (k 2 tog, y fwd) 8 times, k 2 tog.

Next row; yrn, to make one st, then p.

Work 2 more rows in ss and cast off. Fold the cast off edge up, across the row of holes, to make a hem and sl st this in place. This is the lower edge of the hair. Sew this in place from one side of the face to the other leaving a bald patch on top.

BEARD AND FACE

With the same yarn and No14/2 mm needles, cast on 10sts and work in single rib for 1 in/5 cm. Now dec one st at each end of every alt row until only 2 sts rem. K 2 tog and darn the end into the beard.

Embroider the large pink nose and blue eyes, then sew the beard in place, placing a couple of sts into the hair at each side.

Sew the hat on to the head all the way round.

Troll

The troll is a Scandinavian-type creature, sadly misshapen, who lives in deep forests, mountains and under bridges. Remember the story of Billy-Goat Gruff? This one has blue skin to make him appear less human! The body framework will have to be adapted somewhat, but the diagram gives the rough size and shape of the figure without clothes. Pad and wrap it to form this bulky appearance, and make a blue skin cover instead of a pink one. The (bare) blue feet and breeches are knitted all in one piece, as are the body and head covering. Over this, he wears a dark hooded waistcoat. The hands and sleeves are also made all in one piece, see photo on page 83.

FEET AND BREECHES

With light-blue 3 or 4 ply yarn and No13/2¼mm needles, begin at the toe end, cast on 8sts and work 14 rows in ss; now change to mid-blue and work 2 rows. Now inc 1st at each end of the next 2 k rows, (12sts). Work straight until there are 14 mid-blue rows, then

cast off and make another piece the same. These are the leg and breeches pieces. Sew them up as far as the top of the leg, insert the legs and then continue to sew the front and back seams.

TUNIC AND HEAD COVER

With mid-blue 3 ply yarn and the same needles, cast on 26sts and work in ss for 8 rows. Divide for the armholes as follows: work on the first 7sts, for 7 rows, then break off the yarn and join to the next section. Work on these 12sts for 7 rows. Break the yarn off again and work on the last 7sts for 7 rows, then p across all 26sts and then p one more row. Change to light-blue and p the next row.

Next row; (k 2, k 2 tog) 6 times, k 2.

Work 9 more rows in ss and draw the last row up on to a thread to form the top of the head.

Sew down the back from the top of the head to the waist, then run a gathering thread round the neck and draw up firmly. Sew the lower edge of the tunic to the breeches.

Sleeves

Cast on 12sts (mid-blue) and work 14 rows in ss. On the 15th row, p instead of k. Change to light-blue yarn and work 3 rows in ss beginning with a p row.

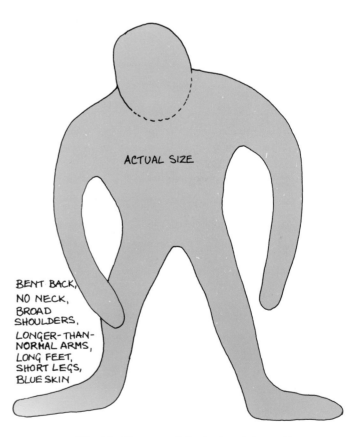

ACTUAL SIZE

BENT BACK,
NO NECK,
BROAD
SHOULDERS,
LONGER-THAN-
NORMAL ARMS,
LONG FEET,
SHORT LEGS,
BLUE SKIN

Fig 42: diagram of the body of the troll

Next row; (k 2 tog, k 3) twice, k 2 tog, (9sts).
Continue in ss for about 13 rows, or until the required length. Do not cast off, but draw the stitches up and sew the side seam, slip on to the arm and stitch to the tunic armhole. Make 2.

BEARD, HAIR AND FACE

Using No14/2 mm needles and white DK yarn, cast on 5sts and knit 5 rows in moss st then cast off. Sew the beard on to the bottom of the face, pulling the two sides up towards the ears. Embroider the hair with the same yarn, then embroider the features.

HOODED WAISTCOAT

Begin with the back piece, and with dark-blue yarn cast on 16sts and work 20 rows in ss.
Row 21; (k 2 tog, k 5) twice, k 2 tog
Row 22; p 13.
Row 23; k 2 tog, k 4, k 2 tog, k 3, k 2 tog.
Row 24; p 10.
Break off the yarn and leave these sts on a spare needle or stitch-holder. For the right front, cast on 10sts and work in ss except for the last 2sts on every p row which should be knitted. Continue straight for 20 rows.
Row 21; k 8, k 2 tog.
Row 22; p 7, k 2.
Row 23; k 7, k 2 tog.
Row 24; p 6, k 2.
Break off yarn and slip these sts on to a stitch-holder. For the left front, work as for the right front except that the 2 gt sts should be worked at the *beginning* of every p row instead of at the end. Reverse all shapings.
Now place all the stitches held on stitch-holders, in order, on to one needle and k across R front, back, and L front, beginning as follows:
Next row; cast off 4sts, k to end.
Next row; cast off 4sts, p to last 2sts, k 2.
Work on these 18sts for the hood for 12 more rows, keeping a border of gt s at each edge. Cast off, fold the hood in half across the top and sew together. Sew half-way up the side edges, leaving the open part for the arms.

STICK

Twist two pcs tightly together. Bend the doubled ends over at the top and bottom, and wrap tightly with brown yarn.

Dragon

In spite of great efforts on my part to make a really fearsome dragon, this dear little harmless creature emerged, and now the other characters are by no means afraid of him, as they were meant to be! However, I feel that he fits into the scene rather well, and he is not difficult to make. As frame sizes may differ in the making, use a tape-measure to check measurements at all stages, and alter the pattern accordingly, see photo on page 87.
You will need No15/1½ mm, No13/2¼ mm and No12/2¾ mm needles; about 1oz/20gms bright orange 3 or 4 ply glittery yarn for the eyes; about 14pcs, sticky-tape, small pliers, strong bendable wire about 14 in/36 cm long, padding; 2 large cup-shaped sequins and 2 small glass beads for the eyes.

FRAME

(These numbers refer to those in Fig 43.)
1. Take 2 pipe cleaners, twist them together, fold in half at right angles as shown.
2. 2 more pcs twisted together 1½ in/4 cm from the left.
3. Place this twist at ⁺ in diagram No 4, and twist short ends round neck.
4. Strengthen back and neck with 2 more pcs laid alongside and twisted.
5. Use 2 pcs double, fold in half, place over body at base of neck for front legs and wrap round to hold in place. Twist legs to strengthen, and turn ends up.
6. Use 2 more pcs and do the same for the back legs, but make them shorter than the front.
7. Bow the legs wide apart and stand evenly.
8. Lengthen tail by twisting 2 pcs tog, and wrapping one end round the end of the body. Dragon frame should now measure about 9½ in/24 cm from the base of neck to tip of tail.
9. Lengthen head by folding 2 more pcs in half and overlap on to the neck by ¾ in/2 cm and bind in place with sticky-tape.
10. Bandage whole frame with long narrow strips of padding, making it thicker round the chest. Wrap in place with yarn.

KNITTED COVER

Main piece
Begin at the nose, and with size No13/2¼ mm needles cast on 12sts and work in gt s for 4 rows, then work 3 rows in ss.
Row 8; inc, k 5, inc, k 4, inc, (15sts).
Row 9; p.
Row 10; inc in every alt st to make 22sts.
Row 11; k.
Row 12; work in moss st for 10 rows.

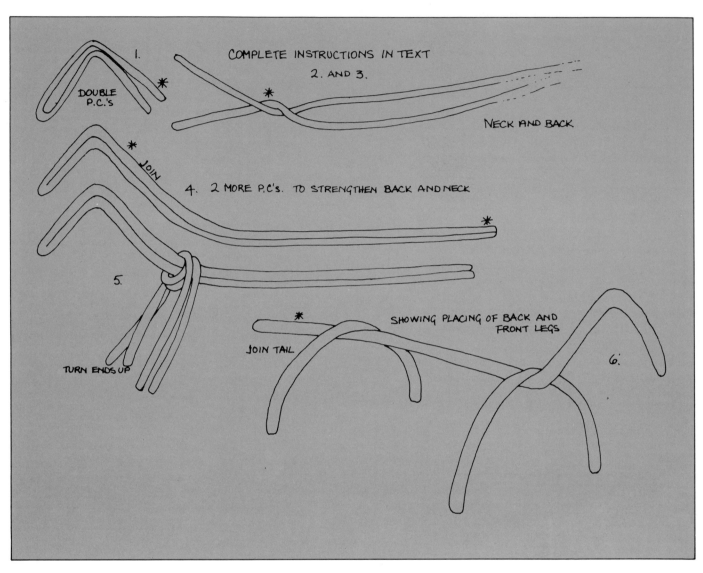

Fig 43: making the wire frame and padding the body of the dragon

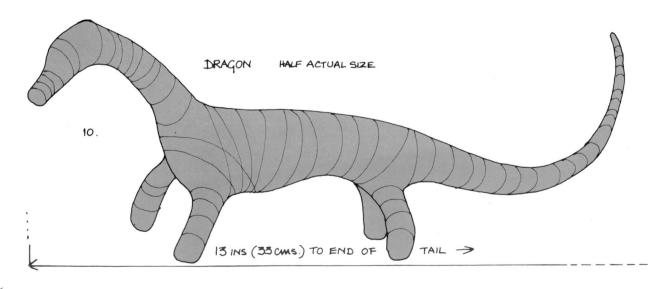

The dragon tries to look fierce but his eyes sparkle like diamonds.

Row 22; work in double moss st for 6 rows.
Row 28; (k 2 tog, work 8sts) twice, k 2 tog, (19sts).
Keeping the patt correct, continue to the base of the neck (about 28 more rows).
Row 57; inc in first st (work 8 sts, inc) twice, (22sts).
Work 2 more rows.
Rows 60 & 61; inc one st at each end of row.
Continue in double moss st for 12 more rows on these 26sts.
Row 74; dec one st at each end of this and every 4th row until 12sts rem.
Work 13 more rows on these 12sts, still in double moss st.
Cast on 3sts * at beg of next 2 rows and change to single moss st.
Work 4 rows without shaping on these 18sts.
Dec one st at each end of next and every foll 4th row until 10sts rem, and continue in moss st until this is nearly long enough to reach the tip of the tail, then dec one st at each end of alt rows until there are 2sts left. Cast off.
Gather the cast on sts on to a thread and draw up tightly. Sew the head up for about 1½ in/4 cm and sew up the same length at the tail end. Slip both ends on to the frame, leaving the yarn uncut so that sewing can continue later.

Legs and underside gusset
Begin at the neck end, and with size No12/2¾ mm needles cast on 2sts. Work in ss, inc one st at each end of every alt row until there are 12sts. Cast on 8sts at beg of next 2 rows, (28sts). Work 12 more rows, then

cast off 8sts at beg of next 2 rows. Continue in ss for 24 rows, or until this piece is long enough to reach the back legs.
For the back legs, cast on 8sts at beg of next 2 rows.
Next row; k 13, k 2 tog, k 13.
P alt rows and dec one st in the centre of every k row until 21sts rem.
[Note: on every alt decrease row, there will be an uneven number of sts at each side of the decrease sts.]
Cast off 8sts at beg of the next 2 rows, then cast off the last 5sts.
Fold the 4 legs in half (downwards) RS together, and sew up the leg seams. Turn RS out and slip these on to the dragon framework, pinning the neck point and the 2 sides in position. Twist the leg seams slightly towards the back. Match up the edges of the upper and lower pieces and pin together along both sides. These must be sewn up while on the framework, from the RS, so care must be taken to make the sts as invisible as possible. Pin the 3 extra sts * underneath the base of the tail, and sew (see Fig 44).

WINGS
With size No15/1½ mm needles, cast on 4sts and work 4 rows in single rib. Now inc at the beg of every alt row until there are 14sts. Work 1 more row and then cast off in rib. Make 2.
Take a piece of strong but bendable wire 7 in/18 cm long and fold it in half, pinching the bend with pliers and gently twisting the rest together. Bend this piece into a right angle, and lay this alongside the right angle of the knitted piece. Using the same yarn, bind the

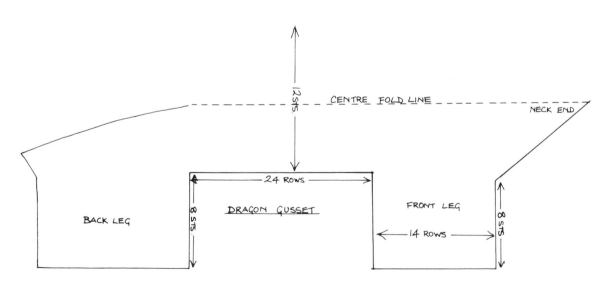

Fig 44: diagram of the underside gusset

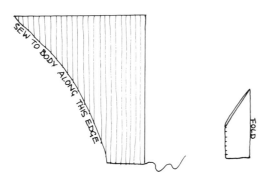

Fig 45: diagrams of the dragon's wings and ears

wire to the edge of the knitting, covering the wire completely with yarn. Sew these wings to each side of the body at the shoulders, (see Fig 45).

EARS

With size No15/1½ mm needles, cast on 8sts and work in ss for 4 rows. Dec one st at each end of every k row until only 2sts rem. Cast off. Make 2. Fold ears along centre line and sew up the 2 short edges, leaving the tops open. Point the ears towards the front, pin on to head and sew firmly.

EYES

Using glittery (or other contrasting) yarn, and size No15/1½ mm needles, cast on 8sts and work in gt s for enough rows to make a ¾ in/2 cm square. Cast off. Make 2. Place a small piece of padding in the centre and gather the edges round the padding and press flat. Sew these pads to each side of the head and finish off with a large cup-shaped sequin held on with a small glass bead.

Unicorn

This beautiful and mythical creature is more the size of a pony than a horse, and differs from the latter in several ways, (see Fig 46). Apart from its spiral horn, it has a goat's beard, cloven hooves like a deer, and a lion's tail. This knitted version has hooves of gold as they are too small to show the cloven effect, see photo on page 91.

You will need No14/2 mm and No12/2¾ mm needles and a small crochet hook to hook the mane into the neck; 4 ply cream or white (less than 1oz/20 gms) and tiny amounts of pink and blue yarns, and metallic gold for the hooves. Some fine glitter yarn may be knitted in

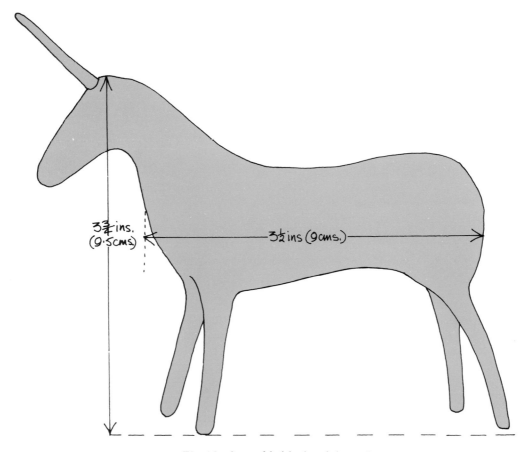

Fig 46: the padded body of the unicorn

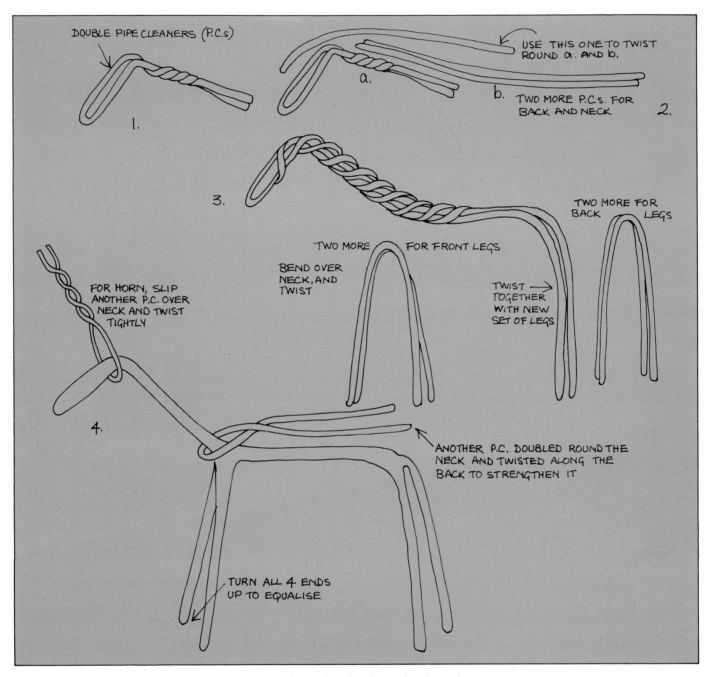

Fig 47: making the wire frame for the unicorn

for the horn, and into the mane. For the frame you will need about 11 pcs, padding and thick white yarn for wrapping, (see Fig 47).

KNITTED BODY COVERING

Front legs

*Using No14/2 mm needles and gold yarn for the hooves, cast on 8sts and k 4 rows in gt s then change to white yarn and k 1 row.

Change to size No12/2¾ mm needles and work in ss* for 12 more rows.

Now cast on 2sts at beg of next 2 rows. Cast off. Make 2. Sew up the seams and slip the leg coverings in place, turning the seam towards the back.

Back legs

Work from * to * as for the front legs then work for 16 more rows, and finish in the same way as for the front legs. Make 2.

Body covering

Use size No12/2¾ mm needles and white yarn, and begin at the nose end.

The unicorn is a mythical creature
who has dainty golden hooves and sparkling eyes

Cast on 12sts and work in ss for 2 rows, then inc at each end of every k row until there are 18sts, ending with a p row. Now make a hole for the horn (you may have to adjust the placing of this).

Next row; inc in first st, k 7, cast off 2, k 7, inc in last st.
Next row; p 9, turn and cast on 2sts, turn and p 9.
Continue increasing in first and last sts until there are 24sts then p the next row.

Shape neck

Inc in first st, k 13, leave 10sts on LH needle, turn and p 4. Turn and k 6, turn and p 8, turn and k 10, turn and p 12, turn and k 14, turn and p 16, turn and k to last st, inc one st. Now p across all sts.
Continue to inc as before until there are 30sts, then work straight for 9 more rows.
Next row; k 2 tog, (k 12, k 2 tog) twice.
Continue without shaping for 12 rows.
Next row; inc in first st, (k 12, inc) twice.
Next row; k 18, turn, leaving 12sts on LH needle, p 6, turn and k 9, turn and p 12, turn and k 15, turn and p 18, turn and k to the end of the row. Now p one more row.
Next row; k 2 tog across all sts (15sts).
Next row; p 15.
Gather these 15sts on to the attached yarn and draw up.

MAKING UP

1. First attach the leg coverings, keeping the seams of the front ones towards the back, and those on the back ones towards the insides. Stitch the top edges to the body-padding, pulling them high on to the body with the stitches.

2. Gather the nose-end (i.e. the cast on edge) of the body-covering and secure with one or two stitches, then sew neatly along the under-head/neck seam as far as the increases. This is the lower point of the chest, at the top of the two front legs.

3. Slip this part on to the frame, slipping the horn through the hole in the head part. Fit it snugly on to the head and chest, and pull the back curve over the back end of the body. Bring the two gathered edges together under the body at the top of the two back legs, and pin in position. Draw the edges together under the rest of the body, round the front legs, and pin. Sew neatly in position.

4. The horn should now be trimmed to about 1¼ in/ 3 cm long and a cover knitted using a fine 3 ply yarn or a fine metallic yarn. Use size No14/2 mm needles and cast on about 8–10sts and knit the length of the horn, tapering towards the end. Sew, from the point downwards, inserting the horn when only about half has been sewn up so that the lower half can be sewn and shaped 'in situ'. Sew firmly in position.

5. The ears are made from the same yarn as the body, using fine needles on about 5sts. Work 4 rows of ss then k 2 tog, k 1, k 2 tog, and on the next row, p 3, then k 2 tog, k 1, and cast off.

6. The tail should be more like a lion's tail than a horse's and so can be a knitted strip with a tassel sewn on to the end. Sew it well up on to the top of the rump.

7. The mane is made up from short lengths of yarn hooked through the sts along the top of the neck. Make this as thick as possible, and if it will not lie down as a mane should, it is probably better to allow it to stand up.

8. The beard, like a goat's, is just a cluster of threads hooked underneath the chin.

9. Embroider the eyes and pink nostrils as shown.

Ladybird

Ladybirds and other beetles, grasshoppers and butterflies are all used by the fairies in the same way that humans use horses. A ladybird can easily carry two or three fairies.

Double knitting yarn is used for the ladybird; small amounts of red and black are required, some firm wire for the legs and two black beads or buttons for the eyes. Small pieces of card are needed for the stiffening and base. Padding is also needed.

Use size No11/3 mm needles, cast on 30 sts in red yarn. Work 28 rows in ss.
Change to black and work 2 more rows, then (k 2 tog, k 3) 6 times.
Purl the next row, then (k 2 tog, k 2) 6 times (18sts).
Continue in ss for 9 more rows, gather the last sts on to a thread and draw up tightly. Stitch the gathers together and pull this section over the head end of the card base. Gather the cast-on edge, stitch together, and pull this over the tail end. Pad between the card and the knitting, and lace across the back.
The legs are made from three pieces of wire each measuring about ⅞ in/8 mm long. These pieces are wrapped with black yarn and bent over at the ends as shown in the diagram. They are stitched on to the underside slightly towards the head end, and the smaller base card is then stuck over the top.

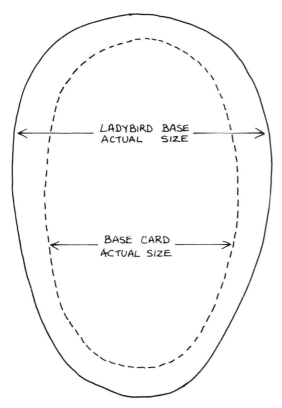

Fig 48: the base for the ladybird body

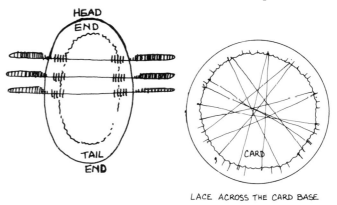

LACE ACROSS THE CARD BASE

Fig 49: completing the ladybird's body and legs

This is by no means the end of the story.
The enchanted characters illustrated here are only
a few of those who may be encountered by mortals,
and their individual appearance will vary greatly
depending on their place of origin.
Every fairy tale will give a different description.
The solution is to take the essential ingredients of
the characters and then use your imagination
as I have done in this book. Use the basic shapes
to create your own fantasy story. It will give great
pleasure to your friends and help to rekindle a
world of magic and fun.

Helping hand

If you are a complete beginner at knitting, or your skills are a little rusty, the following information will be helpful.

Place the needle holding the stitches in the left hand and hold the working needle and the yarn in the right hand. Control the yarn by winding it round the fingers of the right hand, (see Fig 50).

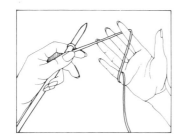

Fig 50 controlling the yarn tension

CASTING ON

Begin with a slip loop about 15 cm (6 in) from the end of the yarn and tighten it on to the left-hand needle (see Fig 51). Insert the right-hand needle into the front of the loop, left to right, wind the yarn round the right-hand needle point and draw it through to the front (see Figs 52 and 53). Transfer the loop from the right-hand needle to the left-hand needle. Continue in this way, but insert the needle *between* the stitches on the left-hand needle, (see Fig 54), until you have the correct number of stitches.

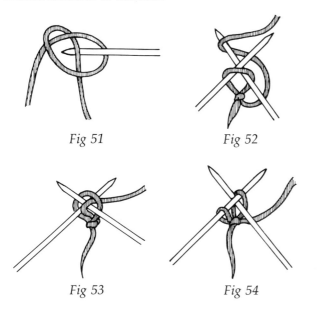

Fig 51   *Fig 52*

Fig 53   *Fig 54*

TO KNIT STITCHES

Hold the yarn at the back of the work. Insert the right-hand needle into the first stitch on the left-hand needle from front to back, left to right (see Fig 55). This is known as 'knitwise'. Pass the yarn round the right-hand needle point, (see Fig 56) and draw the loop through to the front of the work, (see Fig 57). Slip the stitch off the left-hand needle (see Fig 58). Continue in this way along the row until you have transferred all the stitches to the right-hand needle. Turn the work and hold it in the left hand in preparation for the next row.

Knit stitch

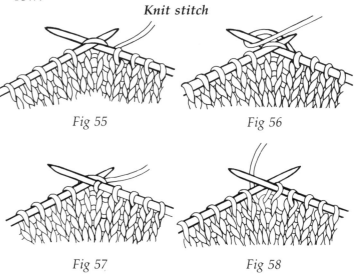

Fig 55   *Fig 56*

Fig 57   *Fig 58*

TO PURL STITCHES

With the yarn at the front of the work, insert the right-hand needle into the front of the first stitch on the left-hand needle from right to left (see Fig 59). This is known as 'purlwise'. Pass the yarn round the right-hand needle point (see Fig 60). Draw the loop through (see Fig 61), then slip the stitch off the left-hand needle (see Fig 62). Continue in this way along the row.

Purl stitch

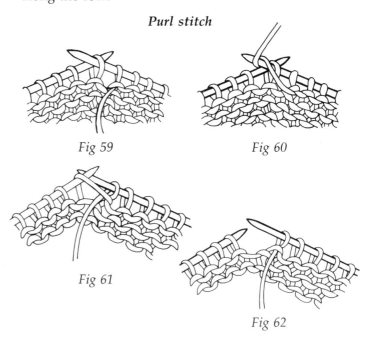

Fig 59   *Fig 60*

Fig 61

Fig 62

Index

Abbreviations 11
Animals 14, 16, 20, 23–25, 27–36,
   85–93

Baby 26
Brownie husband 76, 77
Brownie wife 77, 78
Buildings 16, 17
Bushes
  pom-pon 55, 62, 83

Card 10, 16, 39
Casting on 94, 95
Castle, see 'Enchanted castle'
Cat 55, 56
Children 26, 27, 36
Cows 10, 32, 33

Daffodil elf 70, 71
Daisy elf 69
Dog 20, 25, 26, 31, 32
Donkey 22, 35
Dragon 85–89
Ducks 27

Elves 69–73
Enchanted castle 9, 10, 37–58
  how to make 38–41
Eyelet rib 42

Fairies 65–69
Farmer 16, 22, 29, 33
Farmer's wife 13, 16, 22–24
Farmyard 11–36
Fat goblin 81, 82
Father 20
Fields 15, 16, 23, 31
Figures 18–26, 42, 43, 64–84
  how to make 18, 19, 42, 43
Flowers 16, 34

Forest elf 71, 72

Gnome husband 74, 75
Gnome wife 74–76
Goblin, fat 81, 82
Goblin, thin 80, 81

Hens 13, 28, 36
Horses 10, 37, 45, 48–54

Kitten 23, 28, 29
Knight 10, 47–49
Knit, to 94, 95

Ladybird 70, 92, 93
Landscape 14
Leprechaun 65, 79, 80

Magic forest 59–93
Materials 9
Mother 20
Mule 24, 35

Needles 9

Oberon 65, 67

Padding 10
Pigs 10, 29
Picot pattern 68
Pipe cleaners 10, 18, 19, 42, 43, 50,
  56, 86, 90
Plants 16
Pony 9, 34
Prince 44
Princess 10, 45, 46
Purl, to 94, 95

Rabbit 36
Rug 14

Rumpelstiltskin 82–84

Sheep 16, 30
Sizes 9, 10
Snowflake fairy 68, 69
Stable 29
Stitches 11
  eyelet rib 42
  knit, to 94, 95
  picot pattern 68
  purl, to 94, 95
  satin stitch 14
  tent stitch 14
  tufting 14
Symbols 11

Tension 10
Thin goblin 80, 81
Titania 65, 66
Toadstools
  house 62, 71, 77, 79
  small 63, 68
Tools 9
  farm 31
Trees 16, 23, 26, 36, 37
  talking 38, 60–62
  small 62
  blossom 57
Troll 83–85

Unicorn 11, 37, 89–92

Water elf 72–73
Wings, fairy 66, 67
Witch 38, 54, 55
Wizard 57, 58

Yarns 9

OTHER KNITTING TITLES

HAVE YOU ANY WOOL?
The Creative Use of Yarn
by Jan Messent

A wealth of original and fun ideas are illustrated in this book as Jan Messent shows how oddments of yarn can be used to create a variety of unusual woolly toys and objects. Basic knitting and crochet stitches and shapes are magically transformed into fairytale characters, landscapes, fruit and vegetables, animals and tapestries. Children will delight in the bewitching princess and the pea and the simple card wrapping techniques, while adults will find inspiration in this rich new world of texture and colour.

WOOL 'N MAGIC
by Jan Messent

Wool 'n Magic gives a completely new slant on knitting, crochet and embroidery. You can use your skills to make unique garments and items, combining all three techniques and discover a world of texture, fabric and colour to delight your imagination. Within these pages you will also find ideas and designs for picture knitting, a patchwork town and landscapes, colour experiments using nature as a source and many more fascinating projects.

TRADITIONAL ISLAND KNITTING
by Pam Dawson

This book explores the earliest beginnings of knitting, its origins, history and customs, followed by twenty-six traditional and modern designs from the Channels Islands, the Aran Islands, the Shetlands, Fair Isle, Iceland and the Falklands. Each design is given in sizes suitable for men and women and is accompanied by clear and concise instructions and colour photographs, as well as a 'Helping Hands' section for both the basic and more specialised stitches.

THE CRAFT LIBRARY SERIES

A wide range of traditional and more recent crafts are covered in this series of small paperback books. The series includes a number of knitting books which are listed below.

KNIT THE CHRISTMAS STORY
by Jan Messent

This Nativity scene can be made from the simplest materials by beginners and more experienced knitters. The three-dimensional figures stand about eight inches (20cm) tall and are made from simple rectangles of knitting shaped over heavy card pieces with standing bases. The familiar and well-loved figures are all there, with angels, shepherds, sheep, ox and ass, and the three kings worshipping round the crib with Mary and Joseph.

KNITTED CATS
by Joy Gammon

From the three basic patterns shown in this book you can create your own version of the ideal pet. Whether your preference runs to a macho moggie, or a sophisticated Siamese, these fluffy knitted felines make wonderful toys, cushions and companions.

KNITTED DOGS
by Joy Gammon

Knit a sheepdog, or a shaggy Afghan. Cuddle up with a loveable mongrel. The choice of breed, size and colour is all yours. From three basic patterns you can knit as many as you like. If you get overrun they make marvellous presents.

If you are interested in the above books or any other of the art and craft titles published by Search Press please send for a free colour catalogue to:
Search Press Ltd, Dept B, Wellwood, North Farm Road, Tunbridge Wells, Kent TN2 3DR.